Leading with HQ:

[A Comprehensive Guide to Human Leadership]

ANURAG RAI MBPsS

Organisational Psychologist and Leadership Expert

www.amhwal.com

Leading with HQ

Copyright © 2024 AMHWAL Academy Ltd

All Rights Reserved. No part of this book may be reproduced or utilised in any form or by any means, digital, audio, or printed, without the author's written consent.

The author of this book does not dispense medical advice or prescribe the use of any technique as a form of treatment for physical or medical problems. Please consult with a physician or doctor if you have a medical condition. The information provided is solely on extensive experience and research. The actual results may vary from person to person.

AMHWAL ACADEMY

www.amhwal.com

CONTENTS

	Acknowledgement	3
	Who is this guy?	4
	Introduction	6
CHAPTER 1	Understanding HQ	8
CHAPTER 2	The Cognitive Dimension of HQ	15
CHAPTER 3	The Behavioural Dimension of HQ	32
CHAPTER 4	Three Foundations of Mental Health	44
CHAPTER 5	The Interpersonal Dimension of HQ	49
CHAPTER 6	Introducing the LEADER Framework©	56
CHAPTER 7	Crafting Your Personal Leadership Brand	60
CHAPTER 8	Trust in Leadership - The Three Circles Approach	67
CHAPTER 9	Practical Strategies for Enhancing HQ	72
CHAPTER 10	Case Studies of Leading with HQ	83

CHAPTER 11	Research evidence supporting the principles of HQ	89
CHAPTER 12	Conclusion and Final Thoughts	92
CHAPTER 13	Implementing HQ in Your Leadership Journey	97
CHAPTER 14	The Future of Leadership and HQ	105

BONUS CHAPTERS

CHAPTER 15	Introducing The Human Intelligence Model©	113
CHAPTER 16	Leadability - The Foundation of Effective Leadership	117
CHAPTER 17	Psychological Safety: The Essential Environment for Thriving Teams	121
CHAPTER 18	What is your Leadership Style?	129

APPENDICES

Appendix 1	Resources for enhancing your HQ	151
Appendix 2	Further Guides and Resources for Effective Leadership	165

Acknowledgement

This book is dedicated to you, the reader. I want to thank you. Not just for the money you invested, but also for your trust, commitment, and time you will be investing. I appreciate it, and I don't take it lightly. My goal is to serve you as powerfully as possible in this book. And hopefully make this a thought-provoking, insightful and transformational read. Let's get started.

Loving you

Anurag

Who is this guy?

Let's start by answering the first question first, especially for those of you who don't know me. I am just an ordinary guy who gets to show extraordinary leaders like yourself, how extraordinary they really are. I do not like talking about myself, but I know some of you may be interested in my credentials, so here they are. I am an MSc in Applied and Organisational Psychology, a Certified Master NLP Practitioner, Best Selling Author of the book The Power Within and Mind 2.0, and a multiple times Award-Winning Coach. My work has been featured in major publications such as Fox News, USA Today, Yahoo Finance and MarketWatch.

My clients include Sports personalities, celebrities, police officers, and powerful leaders from all walks of life. I have delivered leadership trainings to small medium and large organisations across the globe.

Here's what some of my clients say about me:

"Anurag brings out the genius within you."

– Graham (CEO of a Technology Firm)

"Anurag's sheer presence and questions... always leave me questioning how I lead my team."

— Jim (Business Owner)

"I can only describe Anurag as someone with magical capabilities at unlocking your potential".

— James (Business Owner)

While I am grateful for all the above, I also know that none of these matters. What matters is what I can do for you. You, the person reading this. My goal with this book is to create a space for you to meet the most extraordinary leader you can become.

Your Biggest Cheerleader

Anurag

Introduction

"Don't let tradition paralyze your mind. Be receptive to new ideas. Be experimental. Try new approaches. Be progressive in everything you do." ~ **David J. Schwartz**

In the dynamic and complex world of the 21st century, leadership demands more than just technical skills or industry knowledge. It requires a deep understanding of human nature, an ability to navigate interpersonal relationships, and a proactive approach to problem-solving. This is where the concept of the Human Quotient, or HQ, comes into play.

HQ is a comprehensive model for leadership that focuses on the ratio of proactive to reactive tendencies in three key areas: cognitive, behavioural, and interpersonal. It provides a framework for leaders to understand and enhance their leadership capabilities, fostering a proactive mindset that can drive innovation, productivity, and success.

This book, "Leading with HQ" aims to provide a complete guide to understanding and implementing the principles of HQ in leadership. It delves into the cognitive, behavioural, and interpersonal dimensions of HQ, providing practical strategies for enhancing these aspects and case studies of successful leaders who exemplify the HQ approach.

We will also explore the role of HQ in leadership development, including its application in training programs and executive coaching. We will look at how organizations can foster a proactive, HQ-based mindset in their leaders, and the benefits this can bring.

In addition, we will examine the evidence supporting the principles of HQ, including research programs like Google's Project Aristotle, and consider the future of HQ leadership in the evolving landscape of the 21st century.

Whether you are a seasoned leader looking to enhance your leadership skills, an aspiring leader seeking to understand the qualities that make a successful leader, or a human resources professional interested in implementing HQ principles in your organization, this book will provide valuable insights and practical guidance.

Join me on this journey to explore the concept of HQ and discover how it can transform leadership for the better. Let's delve into the world of proactive leadership and learn how to lead with HQ.

CHAPTER 1

Understanding HQ

"I'll bet most of the companies that are in life-or-death battles got into that kind of trouble because they didn't pay enough attention to developing their leaders." ~ Wayne Calloway

In the intricate and ever-evolving world of leadership, a fresh metric has emerged, revolutionizing our comprehension of what it truly means to be an effective leader. This metric, known as the Human Quotient or HQ, is a comprehensive model for leadership that provides a robust framework for understanding and enhancing leadership capabilities. But what exactly is HQ, and why is it so critical in today's leadership context? In this chapter, we will delve into the definition of HQ, explore its three key dimensions, and discuss the significance of a proactive versus reactive approach in leadership.

Defining HQ

The Human Quotient, or HQ, is a concept that has been developed to encapsulate a holistic approach to leadership. It is defined as the ratio of proactive to reactive tendencies, providing a measure of a leader's ability to anticipate and shape events rather than just responding to them as they occur.

HQ is not just another buzzword in the leadership lexicon. It represents a paradigm shift in our understanding of leadership, moving away from traditional models that focus primarily on technical skills or industry knowledge. Instead, HQ recognizes that effective leadership requires a deep understanding of human nature, an ability to navigate complex interpersonal relationships, and a proactive approach to problem-solving and decision-making.

In essence, HQ is about the human side of leadership. It's about understanding ourselves and others, about managing our behaviours and interactions, and about shaping our thoughts and actions in a way that drives positive outcomes.

This concept of HQ is a significant departure from traditional leadership models, which often focus on the acquisition of technical skills or industry-specific knowledge. While these elements are undoubtedly important, they do not capture the full range of skills and abilities that a truly effective leader needs. HQ, on the other hand, provides a more holistic view of leadership, one that recognizes the importance of human factors in driving success.

The Three Pillars of HQ

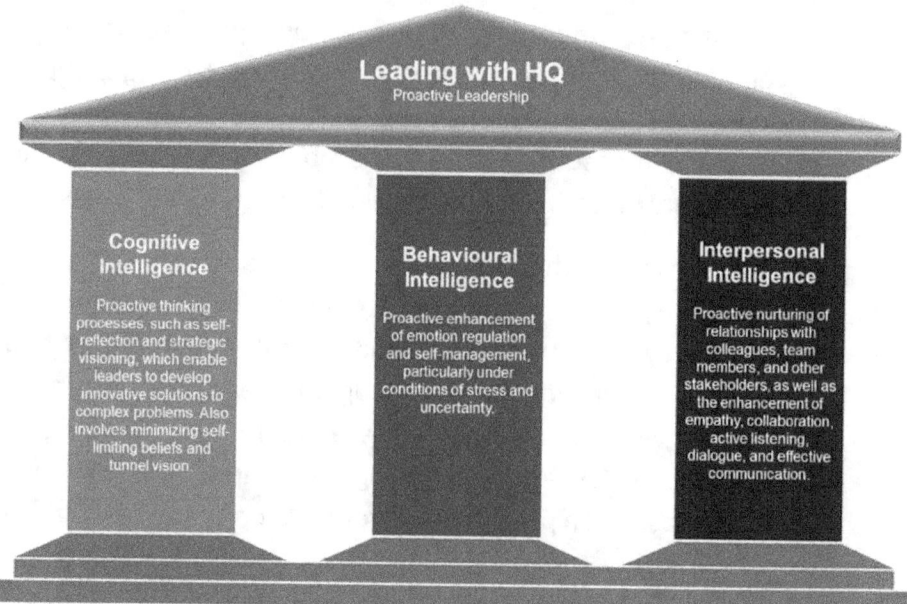

HQ is composed of three interwoven components, each of which plays a critical role in effective leadership. These are the cognitive, behavioural, and interpersonal dimensions.

1. **Cognitive Intelligence**: The cognitive dimension of HQ involves the mental processes that underpin leadership. This includes proactive thinking processes, such as self-reflection and strategic visioning, which enable leaders to understand their own strengths and weaknesses, anticipate future trends, and develop innovative solutions to complex problems. It also involves minimizing self-limiting beliefs and tunnel vision, which can restrict a leader's ability to see the bigger picture or consider alternative perspectives. In

essence, the cognitive dimension is about how leaders think, how they make decisions, and how they strategize.

The cognitive dimension of HQ is not just about having a high IQ or being able to solve complex problems. It's about being able to think strategically, to anticipate future trends and challenges, and to develop innovative solutions that drive success. It's about being able to reflect on one's own strengths and weaknesses, learn from past experiences, and continually strive for improvement. And it's about being able to see beyond the immediate situation, to consider alternative perspectives, and to make decisions that are in the best interests of the organization and its stakeholders.

2. **Behavioural Intelligence**: The behavioural dimension of HQ involves the actions and reactions of leaders. This includes proactive enhancement of emotion regulation and self-management, particularly under conditions of stress and uncertainty. Leaders with high behavioural HQ are able to stay calm under pressure, manage their emotions effectively, and maintain a positive and productive demeanour even in challenging situations. This dimension also involves the elimination of reactive behaviours, such as eye-rolling, raising one's voice, and other manifestations of irritability, which can undermine a leader's effectiveness and damage team morale.

The behavioural dimension of HQ is not just about being able to control one's emotions or maintain a calm demeanour under pressure. It's about being able to manage one's own behaviour in a way that promotes a positive and productive work environment. It's about being able to respond to challenges and setbacks with resilience and determination, rather than with frustration or defeat. And it's about being able to model the kind of behaviour that we want to see in others, setting a positive example for our team members and colleagues.

3. **Interpersonal Intelligence**: The interpersonal dimension of HQ involves the relationships that leaders build with others. This includes proactive nurturing of relationships with colleagues, team members, and other stakeholders, as well as the enhancement of empathy, collaboration, active listening, dialogue, and effective communication. Leaders with high interpersonal HQ are able to build strong, positive relationships, foster a collaborative and inclusive team culture, and communicate effectively with a wide range of people.

The interpersonal dimension of HQ is not just about being able to get along with others or being a good team player. It's about being able to build and maintain strong, positive relationships with a wide range of people, from team members and colleagues to customers and stakeholders. It's about being able to communicate effectively, to listen actively, and to engage in constructive dialogue. And it's about being able to foster a collaborative and inclusive team culture, where everyone feels valued and respected, and where diversity and difference are celebrated rather than feared.

Proactive vs. Reactive Approach

At the heart of the HQ concept is the distinction between a proactive and a reactive approach to leadership. A proactive leader is one who anticipates problems, takes initiative, and assumes responsibility for their actions. They are forward-thinking, strategic, and focused on long-term goals. They don't just react to events as they occur, but actively shape those events to drive positive outcomes.

In contrast, a reactive leader is one who tends to respond to situations as they arise, often driven by immediate circumstances or old habits. While there is a place for reactive leadership, particularly in crisis situations where immediate action is required, an over-reliance on this approach can limit a leader's effectiveness and potential for growth. Reactive leaders can become trapped in a cycle of constant firefighting, with little time or energy left for strategic thinking or proactive problem-solving.

In the following chapters, we will delve deeper into each of these dimensions, exploring practical strategies for enhancing them and providing case studies of successful leaders who exemplify the HQ approach. We will also discuss how HQ can be applied in leadership development, including its role in training programs and executive coaching. By understanding and implementing the principles of HQ, leaders can foster a proactive mindset that drives innovation, productivity, and success.

In essence, HQ is about becoming the best leader you can be. It's about understanding yourself and others, managing your behaviours and interactions effectively, and thinking strategically and proactively. It's about becoming a leader who not only achieves their own goals, but also inspires and empowers others to achieve theirs. And that, ultimately, is what leadership is all about.

In this chapter, we have laid the groundwork for understanding HQ. As we move forward, we will delve deeper into each dimension, providing you with the tools and strategies you need to enhance your HQ and become a more effective leader.

CHAPTER 2

The Cognitive Dimension of HQ

"A leadership culture is one where everyone thinks like an owner, a CEO or a managing director. It's one where everyone is entrepreneurial and proactive." ~ Robin Sharma

The cognitive dimension of HQ is a critical aspect of leadership that involves the mental processes that underpin decision-making, problem-solving, and strategic planning. It is about how leaders think, how they make decisions, and how they strategize. In this chapter, we will delve deeper into the cognitive dimension of HQ, exploring the importance of proactive thinking, the role of self-reflection and strategic visioning, and the need to overcome self-limiting beliefs and tunnel vision.

Understanding the Cognitive Dimension

The cognitive dimension of HQ is a critical aspect of leadership that involves the mental processes that underpin leadership. This includes proactive thinking processes.

The cognitive dimension of HQ is not just about having a high IQ or being able to solve complex problems. It's about being able to think strategically, to anticipate future trends and challenges, and to develop innovative solutions that drive success. It's about being able to reflect on one's own strengths and weaknesses, to learn from past experiences, and to continually strive for improvement. And it's about being able to see beyond the immediate situation, to consider alternative perspectives, and to make decisions that are in the best interests of the organization and its stakeholders.

To truly understand the cognitive dimension of HQ, we must delve deeper into the intricacies of our thought processes. Our minds are complex, capable of processing vast amounts of information and making intricate connections. However, our thought processes can also be influenced by biases, past experiences, and societal norms, which can lead to self-limiting beliefs and tunnel vision.

The cognitive dimension of HQ, therefore, involves not only enhancing our proactive thinking processes but also minimizing these self-limiting beliefs and tunnel vision. It's about expanding our mindset, challenging our assumptions, and opening ourselves up to new possibilities. It's about learning to navigate the complexities of our minds, to harness the power of our thoughts, and to steer our thinking in a direction that leads to effective leadership.

The Importance of Proactive Thinking

At the heart of the cognitive dimension of HQ is the concept of proactive thinking. Proactive thinking involves anticipating future trends and challenges, developing innovative solutions, and taking initiative to drive positive outcomes. It is about being forward-thinking, strategic, and focused on long-term goals.

Proactive thinking is a critical skill for leaders in today's fast-paced and complex business environment. It enables leaders to stay ahead of the curve, to anticipate changes in the market or the competitive landscape, and to take action before problems arise. It also enables leaders to seize opportunities, to innovate, and to drive growth and success for their organization.

Proactive thinking is not just about being proactive in the sense of taking initiative or being assertive. It's about being proactive in the way we think, in the way we approach problems, and in the way we make decisions. It's about being proactive in our learning, in our development, and in our growth as leaders.

In a rapidly changing business environment, the ability to anticipate and adapt to changes is crucial. Leaders who are proactive thinkers are able to foresee potential challenges and opportunities, allowing them to make strategic decisions that keep their organizations ahead of the curve. They are not just reacting to changes as they occur but are actively shaping the future direction of their organizations.

Moreover, proactive thinking involves taking the initiative to drive positive outcomes. Proactive leaders do not wait for opportunities to come to them; they go out and create them.

They are constantly looking for ways to improve, innovate, and drive growth. They take responsibility for their actions and are committed to making a positive impact on their organizations.

Proactive thinking also involves a focus on long-term goals. While it's important to address immediate challenges and short-term objectives, proactive leaders are also thinking about the future. They are considering where they want their organizations to be in five, ten, or even twenty years, and are making strategic decisions to guide their organizations towards these long-term goals.

However, proactive thinking is not something that comes naturally to everyone. It requires a certain mindset, a willingness to take risks, and the ability to think strategically. It requires leaders to step out of their comfort zones, to challenge the status quo, and to embrace change. It also requires ongoing learning and development, as leaders need to constantly update their knowledge and skills to stay ahead of the curve.

The Role of Self-Reflection and Strategic Visioning

Self-reflection and strategic visioning are two key components of proactive thinking that play a critical role in the cognitive dimension of HQ. Both of these elements require a deep level of introspection and forward-thinking, which are essential for effective leadership.

Self-Reflection

Self-reflection involves taking the time to reflect on our own thoughts, feelings, and actions, to understand our strengths and weaknesses, and to learn from our experiences. It enables us to gain insights into our own behaviour, to understand why we do what we do, and to identify areas for improvement. It also enables us to develop self-awareness, which is a critical skill for effective leadership.

Self-reflection is not just about introspection or self-analysis. It's about being present with our thoughts and feelings, observing them without judgment, and accepting them as they are. It's about being curious and open-minded, exploring our inner world with a sense of curiosity and openness. And it's about being compassionate and kind to ourselves, treating ourselves with the same kindness and compassion that we would treat a good friend.

By engaging in self-reflection, leaders can gain a deeper understanding of their own motivations, values, and beliefs. They can identify patterns in their behaviour, recognize their strengths and weaknesses, and uncover potential blind spots. This self-awareness can help leaders to make more informed decisions, to manage their emotions more effectively, and to build stronger relationships with their team members.

Moreover, self-reflection can also promote personal growth and development. By reflecting on their experiences, leaders can learn from their mistakes, celebrate their successes, and continually strive for improvement. They can set personal goals, track their progress, and take responsibility for their own learning and development.

Strategic Visioning

Strategic visioning, on the other hand, involves looking ahead, anticipating future trends and challenges, and developing a clear and compelling vision for the future. It enables us to see the bigger picture, to understand where we want to go and how we're going to get there, and to inspire and motivate others to join us on our journey.

Strategic visioning is not just about setting goals or making plans. It's about creating a vision that is inspiring, compelling, and aligned with our values and purpose. It's about imagining the future we want to create, and then working backwards to identify the steps we need to take to make that future a reality.

Strategic visioning requires a deep understanding of the business environment, a keen sense of foresight, and a strong ability to think critically and creatively. It requires leaders to stay informed about industry trends, market dynamics, and technological advancements. It also requires them to be able to analyse complex information, to make strategic decisions, and to communicate their vision effectively to their team.

By engaging in strategic visioning, leaders can guide their organizations towards a successful future. They can anticipate changes in the market, develop innovative strategies, and align their team around a common goal. They can inspire and motivate their team, foster a sense of purpose and direction, and drive performance and results.

Overcoming Self-Limiting Beliefs and Tunnel Vision

While proactive thinking, self-reflection, and strategic visioning are critical for the cognitive dimension of HQ, it is equally important to overcome self-limiting beliefs and tunnel vision. These cognitive barriers can hinder a leader's ability to think proactively, reflect effectively, and envision strategically.

Self-Limiting Beliefs

Self-limiting beliefs are beliefs that limit our potential, that hold us back from achieving our goals, or that prevent us from seeing the full range of possibilities. They can be beliefs about ourselves, about others, or about the world around us. They can be deeply ingrained, often rooted in past experiences or societal norms, and they can be difficult to change.

For example, a leader might hold the belief that they are not creative enough to come up with innovative solutions, or that they are not charismatic enough to inspire their team. These beliefs can limit a leader's effectiveness, preventing them from fully utilizing their skills and abilities, and hindering their performance and success.

Overcoming self-limiting beliefs requires self-awareness, critical thinking, and a willingness to challenge our own assumptions and beliefs. It requires us to recognize and acknowledge our self-limiting beliefs, to question their validity, and to replace them with more empowering beliefs.

This process can be challenging, as it often involves confronting our fears and insecurities, and stepping outside of our comfort zone. However, by overcoming our self-limiting beliefs, we can unlock our full potential, enhance our cognitive HQ, and become more effective and impactful leaders.

Tunnel Vision

Tunnel vision, on the other hand, is a narrow focus on a particular issue or problem, to the exclusion of other perspectives or possibilities. It can be caused by stress, overload, or a lack of diversity in our thinking or our experiences. It can limit our ability to see the bigger picture, to consider alternative perspectives, or to think creatively and innovatively.

For example, a leader might be so focused on achieving a specific target or goal, that they overlook other important aspects of their role, such as building relationships with their team, or considering the long-term implications of their decisions. This narrow focus can limit a leader's effectiveness, leading to missed opportunities, poor decision-making, and reduced performance and success.

Overcoming tunnel vision requires a broad perspective, an open mind, and a willingness to consider alternative perspectives and possibilities. It requires us to step back from the immediate situation, to see the bigger picture, and to consider the broader context in which we operate. It also requires us to be mindful of our stress levels and workload, and to ensure that we have a diverse range of experiences and perspectives to draw upon.

By overcoming tunnel vision, we can enhance our cognitive HQ, make more informed and balanced decisions, and become more effective and impactful leaders.

In the next sections, we will delve deeper into the strategies and techniques that leaders can use to overcome self-limiting beliefs and tunnel vision, and to enhance their cognitive HQ. We will explore the power of mindful self-reflection, the role of strategic reasoning, the impact of cognitive biases, the power of divergent thinking, and the role of critical thinking.

The Power of Mindful Self-Reflection

Mindful self-reflection is a powerful tool for enhancing the cognitive dimension of HQ. It involves taking the time to reflect on our thoughts, feelings, and actions in a mindful way - that is, with full presence, non-judgment, and acceptance.

Mindful self-reflection allows us to gain a deeper understanding of ourselves, our motivations, and our behaviours. It enables us to identify our strengths and weaknesses, to recognize patterns in our behaviour, and to uncover potential blind spots. It also enables us to learn from our experiences, to make sense of our past, and to plan for our future.

Mindful self-reflection is not just about introspection or self-analysis. It's about being present with our thoughts and feelings, observing them without judgment, and accepting them as they are. It's about being curious and open-minded, exploring our inner world with a sense of curiosity and openness. And it's about being compassionate and kind to ourselves, treating ourselves with the same kindness and compassion that we would treat a good friend.

By engaging in mindful self-reflection, leaders can gain a deeper understanding of their own motivations, values, and beliefs. They can identify patterns in their behaviour, recognize their strengths and weaknesses, and uncover potential blind spots. This self-awareness can help leaders to make more informed decisions, to manage their emotions more effectively, and to build stronger relationships with their team members.

Moreover, mindful self-reflection can also promote personal growth and development. By reflecting on their experiences, leaders can learn from their mistakes, celebrate their successes, and continually strive for improvement. They can set personal goals, track their progress, and take responsibility for their own learning and development.

In the following sections, we will explore how leaders can practice mindful self-reflection, and how this practice can enhance their cognitive HQ. We will also discuss the role of strategic reasoning in proactive thinking, and the need to overcome self-limiting beliefs and tunnel vision, which can hinder mindful self-reflection and limit a leader's effectiveness.

The Role of Strategic Reasoning

Strategic reasoning is another key component of the cognitive dimension of HQ. It involves thinking strategically about the future, considering the potential consequences of different actions, and making informed decisions that align with our long-term goals.

Strategic reasoning is not just about making plans or setting goals. It's about understanding the bigger picture, considering the broader context in which we operate, and making decisions that are in the best interests of our organization and its stakeholders. It's about anticipating future trends and challenges, developing innovative solutions, and driving positive outcomes.

Strategic reasoning requires a deep understanding of the business environment, a keen sense of foresight, and a strong ability to think critically and creatively. It requires leaders to stay informed about industry trends, market dynamics, and technological advancements. It also requires them to be able to analyse complex information, to make strategic decisions, and to communicate their vision effectively to their team.

By engaging in strategic reasoning, leaders can guide their organizations towards a successful future. They can anticipate changes in the market, develop innovative strategies, and align their team around a common goal. They can inspire and motivate their team, foster a sense of purpose and direction, and drive performance and results.

In the following sections, we will explore how leaders can enhance their strategic reasoning skills, and how these skills can contribute to their cognitive HQ. We will also discuss the need to overcome self-limiting beliefs and tunnel vision, which can hinder strategic reasoning and limit a leader's effectiveness.

Overcoming Cognitive Biases

Cognitive biases are systematic errors in thinking that can affect the decisions and judgments that people make. They can be the result of our brain's attempt to simplify information processing, and they can lead to perceptual distortion, inaccurate judgment, or illogical interpretation.

In the context of leadership and HQ, cognitive biases can significantly impact a leader's ability to think proactively, reflect effectively, and envision strategically. They can lead to flawed decision-making, poor problem-solving, and ineffective leadership. Therefore, overcoming cognitive biases is a crucial aspect of enhancing the cognitive dimension of HQ.

There are many different types of cognitive biases, but some of the most common ones that can affect leaders include confirmation bias, anchoring bias, overconfidence bias, and availability bias.

Confirmation bias is the tendency to search for, interpret, favour, and recall information in a way that confirms one's preexisting beliefs or hypotheses. It can lead to flawed decision-making, as it can cause leaders to overlook or ignore information that contradicts their preconceived notions.

Anchoring bias is the tendency to rely too heavily on the first piece of information encountered (the "anchor") when making decisions. It can lead to poor decision-making, as it can cause leaders to give disproportionate weight to initial information and fail to adequately consider subsequent information.

Overconfidence bias is the tendency to overestimate one's own abilities or the accuracy of one's beliefs. It can lead to poor decision-making and risk-taking, as it can cause leaders to underestimate risks and overestimate the likelihood of positive outcomes.

Availability bias is the tendency to rely on immediate examples that come to mind when evaluating a specific topic, concept, method, or decision. It can lead to flawed decision-making, as it can cause leaders to base decisions on information that is readily available, rather than all relevant information.

Overcoming cognitive biases requires self-awareness, critical thinking, and a commitment to evidence-based decision-making. It requires leaders to recognize and acknowledge their biases, to question their assumptions and beliefs, and to seek out diverse perspectives and information. It also requires leaders to create a culture that values and encourages critical thinking, open dialogue, and diversity of thought.

The Power of Divergent Thinking

Divergent thinking is a method used to generate creative ideas by exploring many possible solutions. It involves going beyond the obvious to explore multiple angles and perspectives. Divergent thinking is about generating quantity and variety to give the problem solver multiple possible solutions to choose from.

In the context of HQ, divergent thinking is a crucial skill for leaders. It allows them to see beyond the immediate situation, to consider alternative perspectives, and to generate innovative solutions to complex problems. It's a way of thinking that encourages curiosity, flexibility, and imagination.

Divergent thinking is not just about creativity or innovation. It's about being open to different ideas and perspectives, being willing to challenge the status quo, and being able to see connections and patterns that others might miss. It's about thinking 'outside the box' and not being afraid to take risks or make mistakes.

Divergent thinking requires an open mind, a willingness to challenge the status quo, and a tolerance for ambiguity and uncertainty. It also requires a supportive environment that encourages creativity, diversity, and risk-taking. It's about creating a culture where new ideas are welcomed, where different perspectives are valued, and where everyone is encouraged to think creatively and innovatively.

By fostering divergent thinking, leaders can enhance their cognitive HQ, drive innovation, and lead their organizations towards success. They can generate a wider range of ideas and solutions, make more informed and creative decisions, and foster a culture of innovation and creativity.

The Role of Critical Thinking

Critical thinking is an essential component of the cognitive dimension of HQ. It involves the ability to analyse information objectively, to evaluate different perspectives and arguments, and to make informed decisions based on evidence and logic. Critical thinking enables leaders to solve complex problems, make sound decisions, and develop effective strategies.

Critical thinking is not just about analysing information or solving problems. It's about thinking clearly and rationally, understanding the logical connections between ideas, and identifying, constructing, and evaluating arguments. It's about questioning assumptions, challenging the status quo, and being open to new ideas and perspectives. And it's about making decisions that are logical, well-reasoned, and based on evidence.

In the context of leadership, critical thinking is crucial for effective decision-making and problem-solving. It enables leaders to analyse complex situations, evaluate different options, and make informed decisions that are in the best interests of their organization. It also enables leaders to anticipate potential challenges and risks, develop effective strategies, and drive positive outcomes.

Moreover, critical thinking can also enhance a leader's ability to communicate effectively, build strong relationships, and lead their team successfully. By thinking critically, leaders can articulate their ideas clearly, listen to and understand different perspectives, and build consensus around a shared vision or goal.

However, critical thinking is not a skill that comes naturally to everyone. It requires practice, patience, and a willingness to challenge our own beliefs and assumptions. It requires an open mind, a curious nature, and a commitment to learning and growth.

To enhance critical thinking, leaders can engage in activities such as reading widely, engaging in debates or discussions, solving complex problems, and reflecting on their own thinking processes. They can also seek out diverse perspectives, question their own assumptions, and strive to understand the underlying principles and concepts.

In the following sections, we will explore how leaders can enhance their critical thinking skills, and how these skills can contribute to their cognitive HQ. We will also discuss the need to overcome self-limiting beliefs and tunnel vision, which can hinder critical thinking and limit a leader's effectiveness.

Conclusion

The cognitive dimension of HQ is a critical aspect of leadership that involves the mental processes that underpin decision-making, problem-solving, and strategic planning. It's a complex interplay of proactive thinking, self-reflection, strategic visioning, and the ability to overcome self-limiting beliefs, tunnel vision, and cognitive biases.

By developing proactive thinking, leaders are able to anticipate future trends and challenges, develop innovative solutions, and take initiative to drive positive outcomes. They are able to stay ahead of the curve, seize opportunities, and drive growth and success for their organization.

Through mindful self-reflection, leaders gain a deeper understanding of their own motivations, values, and beliefs. They can identify patterns in their behaviour, recognize their strengths and weaknesses, and uncover potential blind spots. This self-awareness can help leaders to make more informed decisions, to manage their emotions more effectively, and to build stronger relationships with their team members.

Strategic visioning allows leaders to look ahead, anticipate future trends and challenges, and develop a clear and compelling vision for the future. It enables them to see the bigger picture, to understand where they want to go and how they're going to get there, and to inspire and motivate others to join them on their journey.

However, these skills and abilities can be hindered by self-limiting beliefs, tunnel vision, and cognitive biases. These cognitive barriers can limit a leader's effectiveness, leading to flawed decision-making, poor problem-solving, and ineffective leadership. Therefore, overcoming these barriers is a crucial aspect of enhancing the cognitive dimension of HQ.

By overcoming self-limiting beliefs, leaders can unlock their full potential, enhance their cognitive HQ, and become more effective and impactful leaders. They can challenge their assumptions and beliefs, expand their mindset, and open themselves up to new possibilities.

By overcoming tunnel vision, leaders can enhance their cognitive HQ, make more informed and balanced decisions, and become more effective and impactful leaders. They can step back from the immediate situation, see the bigger picture, and consider the broader context in which they operate.

By overcoming cognitive biases, leaders can enhance their decision-making, improve their problem-solving, and become more effective leaders. They can challenge their assumptions and beliefs, seek out diverse perspectives and information, and make decisions based on evidence rather than bias or preconception.

In the next chapter, we will explore the behavioural dimension of HQ, which involves the actions and reactions of leaders, and the importance of emotion regulation and self-management. As we delve deeper into each dimension of HQ, we will provide practical strategies and tools to enhance your HQ and become a more effective leader. So, stay tuned as we continue our journey into the world of leading with HQ.

CHAPTER 3

The Behavioural Dimension of HQ

"Highly proactive people don't blame circumstances, conditions, or conditioning for their behaviour. Their behaviour is a product of their own conscious choice."

~ Stephen Covey

In the journey of understanding the Human Quotient (HQ), we have already explored the cognitive dimension, which primarily focuses on the mental processes that underpin decision-making, problem-solving, and strategic planning. As we continue this exploration, we now turn our attention to the second dimension of HQ – the behavioural dimension.

The behavioural dimension of HQ is a critical aspect of leadership that focuses on the actions, reactions, and overall conduct of leaders. It is not just about what leaders think, but also about how they act and respond, particularly in challenging situations. This dimension encompasses a leader's ability to regulate emotions, manage stress, and exhibit behaviours that contribute positively to the workplace environment and to their own effectiveness as leaders.

The behavioural dimension of HQ is about the outward manifestation of a leader's internal cognitive processes. It is about how a leader's thoughts and feelings translate into actions. It is about how a leader handles stress, how they react to challenges, and how they interact with others. It is about the ability to demonstrate self-control, to manage one's emotions, and to behave in a manner that is consistent with one's values and beliefs.

In this chapter, we will delve into the intricacies of the behavioural dimension of HQ. We will explore the importance of emotion regulation and self-management, the impact of reactive behaviours, and the role of mindfulness and stress management strategies. By understanding and enhancing the behavioural dimension of HQ, leaders can improve their effectiveness, build stronger relationships, and create a positive and productive workplace environment. So, let's embark on this journey of exploration and discovery, and delve into the fascinating world of the behavioural dimension of HQ.

Emotion Regulation and Self-Management

Emotion regulation and self-management are two key components of the behavioural dimension of HQ. They are essential skills that every leader needs to cultivate in order to navigate the complex and often stressful landscape of leadership effectively.

Emotion Regulation

Emotion regulation is about understanding and managing our emotional responses. It's about being able to identify and label our emotions, to understand the triggers that cause these emotions, and to manage our emotional responses in a way that is appropriate and constructive.

Emotion regulation is particularly important in leadership roles, where the pressure and stress can often be high. Leaders are frequently faced with challenging situations and difficult decisions that can trigger strong emotional responses. However, leaders who are able to regulate their emotions can maintain their composure under pressure, make more rational and objective decisions, and respond to challenges in a constructive and effective manner.

Emotion regulation is not about suppressing or ignoring our emotions. Rather, it's about acknowledging our emotions, understanding them, and managing them effectively. It's about being able to experience our emotions without letting them control our actions and decisions.

Self-Management

Self-management, on the other hand, is about controlling our behaviours and actions. It involves setting personal goals, managing our time effectively, staying motivated, and exhibiting self-discipline. It's about being able to manage our resources (such as time and energy), to stay focused on our goals, and to behave in a way that is consistent with our values and beliefs.

Self-management is crucial for leaders, as it enables them to stay productive and effective, even in the face of adversity or stress. Leaders who are able to manage themselves effectively can maintain their focus and productivity, manage their resources efficiently, and achieve their goals successfully.

In the following sections, we will delve deeper into the concepts of emotion regulation and self-management, exploring how leaders can cultivate these skills and how they contribute to the behavioural dimension of HQ. We will also discuss the impact of reactive behaviours and the role of mindfulness and stress management strategies in enhancing the behavioural dimension of HQ.

The Impact of Reactive Behaviours

Reactive behaviours are actions or responses that are driven by our immediate emotional reactions to a situation, rather than by thoughtful consideration or deliberate decision-making. These behaviours can be triggered by stress, frustration, anger, or other strong emotions, and they often occur without much conscious thought or control.

In the context of leadership, reactive behaviours can have a significant impact on a leader's effectiveness, their relationships with their team members, and the overall atmosphere of the workplace. These behaviours can include lashing out in anger, making impulsive decisions, or engaging in defensive or aggressive behaviours in response to criticism or conflict.

Reactive behaviours can create a toxic atmosphere in the workplace, leading to increased stress, decreased morale, and reduced productivity. They can damage a leader's relationships with their team members, undermining trust and respect. They can also harm a leader's reputation, making it harder for them to inspire and motivate their team.

Leaders with high HQ strive to minimize these reactive behaviours. They understand the importance of responding to stressful situations in a thoughtful, deliberate, and constructive manner. They recognize that their actions and reactions can have a significant impact on their team and their workplace, and they strive to manage their emotions and behaviours in a way that promotes a positive and productive work environment.

This is not to say that leaders should suppress or ignore their emotions. On the contrary, emotions are a natural and important part of our human experience, and they can provide valuable information about our needs, values, and perceptions. However, leaders with high HQ understand the importance of managing their emotions and expressing them in a way that is respectful, constructive, and aligned with their values and goals.

In the following sections, we will explore strategies for managing reactive behaviours and enhancing the behavioural dimension of HQ. We will discuss the role of mindfulness and stress management strategies, and we will provide practical tips and tools for managing emotions, reducing stress, and promoting positive behaviours in the workplace.

The Role of Mindfulness and Stress Management

Mindfulness and stress management are two key strategies that can help leaders to enhance the behavioural dimension of HQ. They can help leaders to manage their emotions, reduce reactive behaviours, and promote a positive and productive work environment.

Mindfulness: A Key to Emotion Regulation and Self-Management for Leaders

In the fast-paced and often high-pressure environment of leadership, the ability to regulate emotions and effectively manage oneself is not just an asset but a necessity. Mindfulness, a practice deeply rooted in ancient traditions, has emerged as a powerful tool for leaders aiming to navigate the complexities of their roles with grace and resilience. Far from being just a personal wellness trend, mindfulness offers tangible benefits for emotion regulation and self-management, essential competencies for effective leadership.

Understanding Mindfulness in Leadership

Mindfulness, at its core, is the practice of being fully present and engaged in the moment, with a non-judgmental awareness of one's thoughts, emotions, and sensations. For leaders, the application of mindfulness extends beyond personal tranquillity; it equips them with the clarity and calm needed to make considered decisions, communicate effectively, and inspire their teams.

Enhancing Emotion Regulation

Leadership invariably involves navigating challenging situations, from high-stakes decision-making to managing conflicts within teams. Here's how mindfulness aids leaders in emotion regulation:

- **Increased Awareness of Emotional Triggers**: Mindfulness cultivates an acute awareness of one's internal state, helping leaders recognize their emotional triggers. This awareness is the first step in preventing knee-jerk reactions to stressful or provocative situations.

- **Space Between Stimulus and Response**: Practicing mindfulness creates a mental space where leaders can observe their emotions without immediately acting on them. This pause is critical, allowing time to choose a response aligned with their values and the organization's goals, rather than being led by fleeting emotions.

- **Enhanced Emotional Resilience**: Regular mindfulness practice strengthens emotional resilience, enabling leaders to navigate the ups and downs of organizational life with composure. This resilience fosters a workplace culture that is adaptable, open to change, and able to bounce back from setbacks.

Improving Self-Management

Effective leadership also depends on self-management, the ability to direct and control one's actions and responses. Mindfulness enhances self-management in several key ways:

- **Focused Attention**: In a world rife with distractions, mindfulness helps leaders maintain focus on their goals and the task at hand. This focused attention is essential for strategic thinking, planning, and execution.

- **Reduced Stress Levels**: Mindfulness practices, such as meditation, have been shown to lower stress levels. Lower stress leads to clearer thinking and better health, contributing to more sustained energy and presence for leadership duties.

- **Greater Emotional Intelligence**: Mindfulness fosters emotional intelligence, a critical leadership skill. Leaders who are emotionally intelligent are better equipped to understand and empathize with others, facilitating more effective communication and team dynamics.

Integrating Mindfulness into Leadership

Integrating mindfulness into a leadership style doesn't require extensive time away from work or radical changes in behaviour. It can begin with simple practices:

1. **Start with Short, Daily Practices**: Dedicate a few minutes each day to mindfulness meditation or mindful breathing exercises. This small investment of time can yield significant returns in terms of mental clarity and emotional stability.

2. **Mindful Listening**: Practice being fully present in conversations, giving your undivided attention to the speaker. This not only enhances communication but also strengthens relationships within your team.

3. **Reflective Pauses**: Incorporate brief pauses to reflect before making decisions or responding to emails and messages. These moments of reflection can help

ensure your actions are thoughtful and aligned with your leadership objectives.

Mindfulness, with its profound benefits for emotion regulation and self-management, offers leaders a path to more effective, empathetic, and resilient leadership. By adopting mindfulness practices, leaders can navigate the complexities of their roles with greater ease, fostering environments where creativity, productivity, and wellbeing thrive. In doing so, they not only enhance their own performance but also set a powerful example for their teams, promoting a culture of mindfulness that can transform the entire organization.

Stress Management

Stress management involves using various techniques to manage and reduce stress. This could include physical exercise, relaxation techniques, or cognitive strategies such as reframing negative thoughts. Effective stress management can help leaders to stay focused and productive, even in high-pressure situations.

Stress is a common part of leadership, but it can also be a major barrier to effective leadership. High levels of stress can lead to burnout, decreased productivity, and increased risk of health problems. However, by using effective stress management strategies, leaders can manage their stress levels, maintain their well-being, and enhance their effectiveness as leaders.

What is Stress?

Stress, in its most basic form, is the body's response to perceived threats or demands. Historically, this response was crucial for survival, preparing humans to either fight or flee from physical dangers. However, in the modern world, stress triggers are more likely to be psychological - stemming from concerns over money, job satisfaction, relationships, time management, and future uncertainties. Despite the difference in stimuli, the body's reaction remains the same, often leading to a host of negative health outcomes and diminished quality of life.

The root cause of stress, interestingly, lies not in the external triggers themselves but in the gap between our expectations and reality. When life does not align with our preconceived notions of how things should be, stress ensues. This insight is particularly relevant for leaders, who often operate under the pressure of high expectations and unpredictable challenges.

Two mental models to better manage stress.

Model 1: Practice "Good Thing, Bad Thing, Who Knows?"

This model, inspired by a timeless narrative, emphasizes the subjective nature of our experiences. It suggests that labelling events as strictly good or bad is a choice—a choice that significantly influences our stress levels. Leaders can adopt this perspective to navigate the uncertainties and setbacks inherent in leadership roles. By refraining from immediate judgments and embracing a more open-ended view of outcomes, leaders can maintain equilibrium in the face of adversity, thus reducing stress and focusing on opportunities and learnings.

Model 2: Focus on Your Actions, Not Your Results

Derived from the timeless wisdom of the Bhagavad Gita, this model advocates for a focus on effort rather than outcomes. It acknowledges that while we can control our actions, the results are often subject to factors beyond our control. For leaders, this principle is liberating. It shifts the emphasis from the pressure to achieve specific outcomes to the quality and integrity of their actions. Celebrating effort and dedication, regardless of the outcome, fosters a healthier approach to leadership and reduces stress.

For leaders, managing stress is not merely about personal well-being; it's about setting a tone that promotes resilience, adaptability, and a positive work environment.

Conclusion

The behavioural dimension of HQ is a critical aspect of effective leadership. It involves the actions, reactions, and overall conduct of leaders, particularly in response to stressful situations and interpersonal interactions. By regulating their emotions, managing their behaviours, and minimizing reactive responses, leaders can create a positive workplace environment, build strong relationships with their team members, and enhance their own effectiveness.

Emotion regulation and self-management are key components of the behavioural dimension of HQ. They enable leaders to manage their emotional responses effectively, to stay focused and productive under pressure, and to behave in a manner that is consistent with their values and goals.

Reactive behaviours, on the other hand, can have a detrimental impact on the workplace environment and on a leader's effectiveness. Leaders with high HQ strive to minimize these behaviours, choosing instead to respond to challenges in a thoughtful, deliberate, and constructive manner.

Mindfulness and stress management strategies can play a crucial role in enhancing the behavioural dimension of HQ. They can help leaders to stay calm under pressure, to make more mindful decisions, and to manage their stress effectively.

In the end, the behavioural dimension of HQ is about more than just the actions and reactions of leaders. It's about how leaders manage their internal world – their thoughts, feelings, and emotions – and how they express this internal world through their behaviours. It's about the ability to stay calm under pressure, to respond to challenges with grace and resilience, and to lead with authenticity and integrity.

CHAPTER 4
Three Foundations of Mental Health

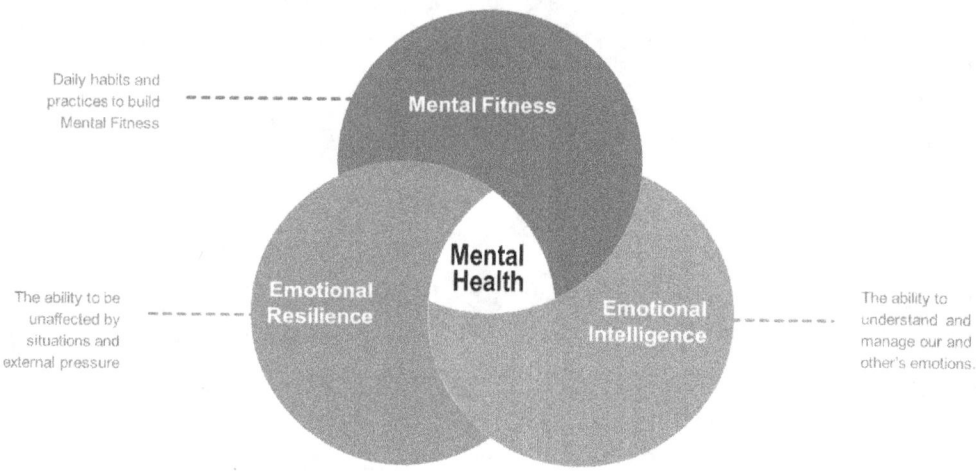

"What mental health needs is more sunlight, more candor, and more unashamed conversation."

~ Glenn Close

Mental health, often overshadowed by physical health, is an integral part of our overall well-being. Like a three-legged stool, it is supported by three critical foundations: Emotional Fitness, Emotional Resilience, and Emotional Intelligence. When one of these legs is weak or missing, our mental health can become unstable. Let's explore these foundations and understand how they contribute to a balanced and healthy mental state.

1. Emotional Fitness

Emotional Fitness mirrors the concept of physical fitness; it's achieved through consistent and daily practice. Just as we exercise our bodies, we must also exercise our minds. Three practices have proven to be exceptionally beneficial for developing emotional fitness:

- **15-20 Minutes of Exercise:** Physical activity is not just good for the body but also for the mind. It can help reduce anxiety, depression, and negative mood by improving self-esteem and cognitive function. It also helps increase better blood circulation to your brain.

- **Meditation:** Meditation helps in calming the mind, reducing stress, and improving focus. Regular meditation can lead to better emotional health by fostering a sense of peace and clarity. Meditation allows us to have better control on our thoughts and so our emotions.

- **Gratitude Journal:** Writing down things for which you are grateful can significantly increase your sense of well-being and happiness. Our brain is designed for survival. So, its natural instinct are to look for what's wrong. This is the reason why 90% of the things in our life are the way we want them to be, yet we focus on the 10% that is not the way we want them to be. Research shows that conscious daily gratitude helps release feel-good chemicals that enable us to be more creative, productive and emotionally intelligent.

2. Emotional Resilience

Emotional Resilience is the ability to bounce back from setbacks, adversity, trauma, tragedy, threats, or significant sources of stress. Having resilience does not mean that you will never feel stressed, worried, angry or any other ineffective emotion. That would be not normal. Expecting that would be like expecting to not feel pain if you injure your knee.

Feeling those emotions means that the system is working fine. So emotional resilience is not absence of these emotion. Resilience is not being affected by the presence of these emotions. And that can only be achieved by detachment. Detachment is not denial.

It's a practice of seeing that our emotions are information and not our identity. Creating the separation that - I feel anger, I am not angry. Just like if you hurt your knee, you have "knee pain", you are not "knee pain". Creating this separation makes us more resilient to the emotion. Acknowledge the emotional and understand that it's okay to feel it. But you do not have to be it. You have a brain; you are not a brain. Building emotional resilience allows us to navigate through difficult emotions and situations with grace and adaptability.

3. Emotional Intelligence

Emotional Intelligence is the capacity to be aware of, control, and express one's emotions judiciously and empathetically. This requires the ability to acknowledge the emotion without labelling it good or bad, positive or negative. And then asking do I want to be feeling this way, if not, then understanding that my thoughts create my feelings. So how can I REFRAME this situation so I have more effective thoughts that will put me into a better emotional state? Self-awareness followed by the ability to reframe our thoughts and perceptions is key to mastering this foundation.

The Interplay of the Three Foundations

Most people face challenges in their mental health journey because they might overlook or undervalue one of these foundations. Each foundation supports and enhances the others. For example, emotional fitness can improve our resilience and intelligence by providing us with the strength and clarity to face and understand our emotions. Emotional resilience allows us to navigate through life's ups and downs with greater ease, while emotional intelligence offers us the tools to manage and express our emotions constructively.

The journey to mental health is continuous and multifaceted. By investing time and effort into developing emotional fitness, resilience, and intelligence, we equip ourselves with the tools necessary for facing life's challenges. Remember, it's not about perfection but progress. Like any form of fitness, the more we practice, the stronger we become.

As we conclude this chapter, I hope that you have gained a deeper understanding of the behavioural dimension of HQ and its importance in effective leadership. In the next chapter, we will explore the third and final dimension of HQ – the interpersonal dimension – which focuses on the relationships and interactions between leaders and their team members. As we delve deeper into each dimension of HQ, I hope to provide you with valuable insights and practical strategies to enhance your HQ and become a more effective leader.

CHAPTER 5

The Interpersonal Dimension of HQ

"A key skill for effective leadership is the ability to enrol people into your vision. Once they have made your vision their own, they do not need to be managed or motivated."

~ Anurag Rai

In our exploration of the Human Quotient (HQ), we have journeyed through the cognitive and behavioural dimensions, understanding how they shape a leader's thought processes and actions. Now, we arrive at the third and final dimension - the interpersonal dimension. This aspect of HQ is the bridge that connects a leader to their team members, stakeholders, and the broader organization. It is the dimension that breathes life into leadership, transforming it from a solitary endeavour to a collective journey.

The interpersonal dimension of HQ focuses on the relationships and interactions between leaders and their team members. It is about how leaders connect with others, how they communicate their ideas and feelings, and how they influence and inspire those around them. It is about the ability to build strong, positive relationships, to communicate effectively, and to foster a collaborative and inclusive work environment.

In the realm of leadership, the interpersonal dimension of HQ is of paramount importance. A leader can have the most brilliant ideas and the most efficient work habits, but without the ability to connect with others, communicate effectively, and foster positive relationships, their leadership potential remains unfulfilled.

In this chapter, we will delve into the intricacies of the interpersonal dimension of HQ. We will explore the importance of building strong relationships, the art of effective communication, and the role of a leader in fostering a positive work environment. We will also provide practical strategies and tools to enhance your interpersonal HQ, enabling you to become a more effective and impactful leader.

So, let's embark on this journey of exploration and discovery, and delve into the fascinating world of the interpersonal dimension of HQ.

Building Strong Relationships

Building strong relationships is a cornerstone of the interpersonal dimension of HQ. It's about more than just working together; it's about fostering a deep sense of connection, understanding, and mutual respect with those around you. This is particularly important in leadership roles, where the ability to build and maintain strong relationships can have a profound impact on a team's morale, productivity, and overall success.

Strong relationships are built on a foundation of trust, respect, and mutual understanding. They require a genuine interest in others, an ability to empathize with their experiences, and a commitment to supporting their growth and development. As a leader, building strong relationships involves understanding the unique strengths, challenges, and aspirations of each team member, and leveraging this understanding to foster a sense of camaraderie and teamwork.

Building strong relationships also involves effective communication. It requires the ability to listen actively and empathetically to express ideas and feedback clearly and respectfully, and to engage in open and constructive dialogue. It also requires the ability to manage conflicts in a constructive manner, to navigate differences of opinion, and to foster a culture of mutual respect and understanding.

Moreover, strong relationships are not built overnight. They require time, effort, and consistency. They require a commitment to ongoing communication, regular feedback, and continuous learning and growth. They require a willingness to invest in others, to support their development, and to celebrate their successes.

Effective Communication

Effective communication is a critical aspect of the interpersonal dimension of HQ. It is the thread that weaves together the fabric of relationships within a team or an organization. It is the medium through which ideas are shared, feedback is given, and consensus is built. In the context of leadership, effective communication is not just a skill, it is a necessity.

Effective communication involves more than just speaking clearly and persuasively. It is a two-way process that involves both speaking and listening, expressing and understanding, talking and observing. It requires the ability to articulate ideas and information in a way that is clear, concise, and compelling. But equally important, it requires the ability to listen actively and empathetically, to understand the perspectives and feelings of others, and to respond in a thoughtful and respectful manner.

In addition, effective communication involves non-verbal cues such as body language, facial expressions, and tone of voice. These non-verbal cues can often convey more information than words alone, and they play a crucial role in building understanding and rapport.

Effective communication also requires emotional intelligence - the ability to understand and manage our own emotions, and to understand and respond to the emotions of others. Leaders with high emotional intelligence are able to communicate in a way that is sensitive to the emotional needs and responses of their team members, and they are able to build stronger and more effective relationships as a result.

Fostering a Positive Work Environment

Creating and fostering a positive work environment is another critical aspect of the interpersonal dimension of HQ. It's about cultivating a workplace culture that promotes respect, collaboration, and mutual support. It's about creating an environment where people feel valued, where their contributions are recognized, and where they are motivated to do their best work.

A positive work environment is characterized by open communication, mutual respect, and a shared sense of purpose. It's an environment where diversity is valued, where everyone feels included, and where differences of opinion are seen as opportunities for learning and growth rather than sources of conflict.

As a leader, fostering a positive work environment involves setting the tone for the workplace culture. It involves modelling the values and behaviours that you want to see in your team, such as respect, integrity, and collaboration. It involves creating opportunities for team members to learn, grow, and contribute, and recognizing their contributions when they do. It also involves addressing conflicts and challenges in a constructive manner and providing support and guidance when needed.

Fostering a positive work environment also involves promoting work-life balance and employee well-being. This can involve providing flexible work arrangements, promoting healthy work habits, and providing support for employees' physical and mental health.

A Magic Potion to Improve Communication, Co-operation, and Culture in your organisation.

Give 5 praises every day to every person you work with professionally and personally for better Communication, Cooperation and Culture.

Three Psychological Principles behind why this works

1. **Pygmalion Effect**: The Pygmalion effect is a psychological phenomenon where higher expectations lead to an increase in performance. Essentially, if someone believes in our potential and expects us to do well, we are more likely to excel. This is the reason why we behave differently in front of different people. If you a friend who thinks that you are a calm person, you are more likely to act calm in their presence. The underlying mechanism is that positive expectations influence interactions and attitudes towards the individual, thereby boosting their confidence and motivation to meet those expectations.
2. **Emotional Bank Accounts**: We all have Emotional Bank Accounts and if the account is in deficit (which most likely is for most people because of our inner critic and critics around us), you cannot make more withdrawals. Technically for every 5 deposits (praises), you can make 1 withdrawal (mention an area for improvement). If we try to withdraw from an emotional bank account that is in deficit, the person is more likely to be defensive than receptive.
3. **The Principle of Reciprocity**: It suggests that people are more likely to and even feel obliged to give back what they receive from you. If I give you praise, you are more likely to give me praise. To give genuine praise you need to look for the good in another person. And to reciprocate they need to look for good in you. Our brain is designed to find more of whatever we are looking for. So, before you realise it, you both start looking for good and so finding more good in each other.

And that's how we change culture and improve relations.

Conclusion

The interpersonal dimension of HQ is a critical aspect of effective leadership. It's about how leaders connect with others, how they communicate their ideas and feelings, and how they influence and inspire those around them. By building strong relationships, communicating effectively, and fostering a positive work environment, leaders can enhance their interpersonal HQ, build a strong and cohesive team, and drive success for their organization.

As we conclude this chapter, we hope that you have gained a deeper understanding of the interpersonal dimension of HQ and its importance in effective leadership. In the next chapter, we will explore practical strategies and tools to enhance your HQ and become a more effective leader. So, stay tuned as we continue our journey into the world of leading with HQ.

CHAPTER 6

Introducing the LEADER Framework©

Transforming Difficult Conversations into Positive Outcomes

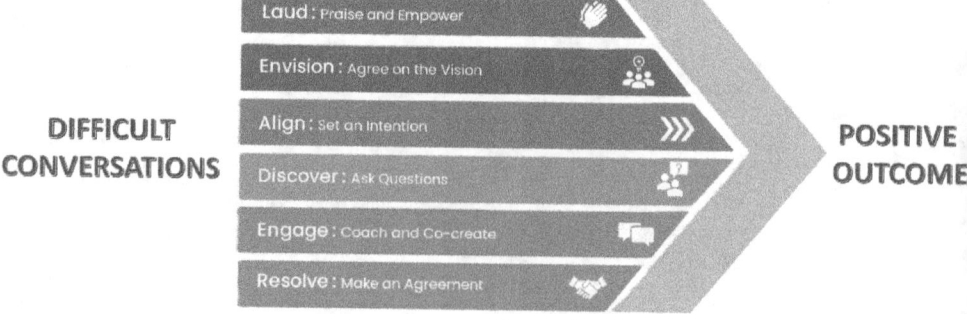

Leader Framework is copyrighted and owned by Anurag Rai and AMHWAL Academy. The use of this framework without attribution is prohibited.

Difficult conversations are an inevitable part of leadership. Whether it's addressing performance issues, navigating conflict, or discussing sensitive topics, the way these conversations are handled can significantly impact organizational culture and outcomes. Recognizing the importance of these discussions, I have developed a powerful approach to not only navigate but also transform difficult conversations into opportunities for growth and positive change: the LEADER framework©.

Laud: Praise and Empower

The LEADER framework begins with "Laud," a critical step that sets the tone for the entire conversation. By starting with praise and acknowledgement, leaders can empower the individual, ensuring the conversation is rooted in respect and mutual appreciation. This approach has three significant benefits:

Establishing a Positive Premise: It reinforces that the discussion isn't about doubting the individual's worth or potential, creating a safe space for open dialogue.

Building the Emotional Bank Account: Positive feedback contributes to the person's emotional resilience, making them less likely to become defensive.

Enhancing Rapport and Likeability: Showing genuine appreciation builds rapport, making the individual more receptive to the conversation.

Envision: Agree on the Vision

Next, "Envision" involves aligning on a shared goal or vision, shifting the focus from problems to shared outcomes. This step is about finding common ground and agreeing on a vision that both parties are committed to achieving. It's a strategic move away from fault-finding to a collaborative stance on future possibilities.

Align: Set Intentions

With a shared vision established, "Align" sets the intention for the conversation. It's about clearly stating the objective and ensuring both parties understand the purpose and goal of the discussion. This clarity lays the groundwork for a productive dialogue focused on achieving the agreed-upon vision.

Discover: Ask Questions

Instead of dictating solutions, "Discover" encourages asking questions that guide the individual to reflect on the most effective ways to achieve the vision. This approach fosters a sense of ownership and empowerment, as it allows the individual to actively participate in finding solutions rather than feeling cornered or criticized. It also helps overcome Psychological Reactance.

Engage: Coach and Co-create

"Engage" takes the conversation a step further by inviting the individual to co-create solutions. Before offering suggestions, it's crucial to seek permission, which respects the individual's autonomy and readiness to receive feedback. This step is about coaching and working together to devise practical steps forward.

Resolve: Make an Agreement

Finally, "Resolve" emphasizes the importance of establishing clear agreements on the next actions. Without clear agreements, the conversation risks being unproductive. This step ensures that both parties have a clear understanding of the expectations and commitments made, laying a solid foundation for accountability and follow-through.

Conclusion

The LEADER framework is a comprehensive approach that transforms difficult conversations from dreaded encounters into opportunities for growth, alignment, and positive change. By following these steps, leaders can navigate challenging discussions with empathy, clarity, and a focus on constructive outcomes. Adopting the LEADER framework can significantly enhance the effectiveness of leadership communication, fostering a culture of open dialogue, mutual respect, and continuous improvement.

Leaders who master the art of difficult conversations using the LEADER framework not only resolve immediate issues but also build stronger, more resilient teams capable of facing challenges with confidence and a collaborative spirit. It's a testament to the power of leadership that is rooted in empathy, vision, and a commitment to collective success.

CHAPTER 7

Crafting Your Personal Leadership Brand

"Your brand is what people say about you when you are not in the room."

~ Jeff Bezos, Amazon

The importance of a personal brand in leadership cannot be overstated. In essence, a personal brand is the unique combination of skills, experiences, and personality that you want the world to see in you. It is how you present yourself to others, and in the realm of leadership, it serves as a powerful tool for influencing, inspiring, and guiding others. Here's why it's so crucial:

1. **Establishes Credibility and Trust**: A well-crafted personal brand helps establish a leader's credibility in their field. When leaders consistently communicate their values, expertise, and experiences, they build trust with their teams, peers, and stakeholders. This trust is foundational for effective leadership, as it encourages others to buy into the leader's vision and direction.

2. **Enhances Visibility and Influence**: A strong personal brand increases a leader's visibility within their industry and beyond. It makes them a go-to resource for insights, advice, and leadership. This visibility can expand their influence, enabling them to impact a larger audience and inspire more people with their vision and values.

3. **Fosters Connections and Opportunities**: Leaders with distinct personal brands often find it easier to network and forge meaningful connections. These connections can lead to new opportunities for collaboration, growth, and innovation, both for themselves and their organizations. A personal brand that resonates with people on a personal level can open doors that might otherwise remain closed.

4. **Differentiates in a Competitive Landscape**: In a world where many leaders may have similar qualifications and experiences, a personal brand helps a leader stand out. It highlights what makes them unique and why they are

the best choice for leading a team or an organization. This differentiation is crucial for advancing in one's career and for attracting top talent to one's team.

5. **Guides Decision-Making and Actions**: A leader's personal brand is a reflection of their core values and principles. It can serve as a guiding light for decision-making and actions, ensuring that they remain true to themselves and their goals. This consistency is key to maintaining the respect and loyalty of followers.

6. **Inspires and Engages Others**: A compelling personal brand not only showcases a leader's strengths but also their human side, including their passions, motivations, and how they overcome challenges. This authenticity inspires and engages teams, fostering a culture where people feel connected to their leader and motivated to contribute to the shared vision.

Building and maintaining a strong personal brand requires intentional effort. It involves understanding your unique value, being consistent in your messaging, engaging with your audience, and being authentic in your interactions. For leaders looking to make a lasting impact, investing in their personal brand is not just beneficial—it's essential.

How To Build a Strong Personal Leadership Brand?

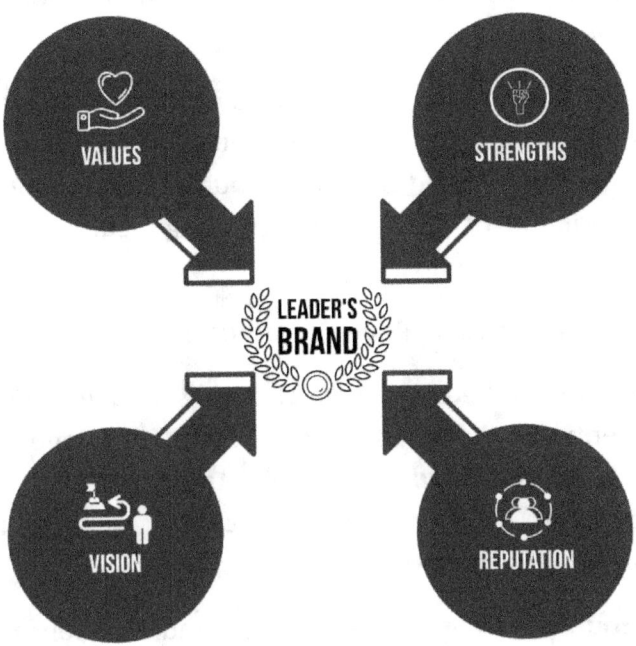

To build and nurture a strong personal brand as a leader, reflecting deeply on these four key areas is essential – Your Values, Your Strengths, Your Reputation, and Your Vision. Each area not only helps you understand and articulate what you stand for but also guides you in communicating your brand authentically and effectively. Let's expand on each of these:

1. Values: The Core of Your Leadership

Reflection: Consider the principles and beliefs that are most important to you. These values shape your decision-making process, your approach to challenges, and how you lead your team.

Ask Yourself: What are the core values and beliefs that guide my leadership style?

Action: Demonstrate your values through your actions. For example, if integrity is a core value, be transparent in your communications and honest in your dealings. Your team and peers will mirror these values, creating a culture that reflects your leadership ethos.

2. Strengths: Your Unique Contribution

Reflection: Reflect on your strengths and experiences that differentiate you. What skills have you developed over your career? Perhaps you excel at strategic thinking, possess exceptional emotional intelligence, or have a knack for inspiring and motivating others.

Ask Yourself: What unique strengths and experiences do I bring to the table?

Action: Leverage these strengths in your leadership role. For instance, if you are adept at problem-solving, lead by example when challenges arise. Offer mentorship and development opportunities that allow you to pass on your skills to others.

3. Reputation: Desired Perception

Reflection: Think about how you want to be perceived by your peers, team, and industry. This encompasses not just your professional capabilities but also your leadership style and interpersonal skills. Do you want to be seen as approachable, a visionary leader, or a change-maker?

Ask Yourself: How do I want to be perceived by my peers, team, and industry?

Action: Actively manage your reputation by being consistent in your words and actions. Engage with your team and peers in a way that reinforces the perception you wish to create. Share your insights and successes through public speaking, social media, and professional networks to build a broader industry reputation.

4. Vision: Your Leadership Legacy

Reflection: Consider the legacy you want to leave and the impact you wish to have on your team and organization. What are your goals for your team and organization? Why are these goals important? Reflecting on your vision can provide a powerful motivational framework for your actions and decisions.

Ask Yourself: What is the destination I am heading to? And why it is important?

Action: Communicate your vision clearly and passionately to your team and stakeholders. Involve them in creating a roadmap to achieve this vision, fostering a shared sense of purpose. Your vision will not only guide your team's efforts but also inspire them to achieve collective goals.

Consistency and Authenticity: The Binding Glue

Consistency in communicating and demonstrating these elements is crucial. Your actions, decisions, and interactions should consistently reflect your values, strengths, desired reputation, and vision.

Authenticity is the foundation of a strong personal brand. Be genuine in your leadership; don't try to adopt a style or values that don't feel true to who you are. People are drawn to authentic leaders, and authenticity fosters trust and loyalty.

In summary, building a personal brand as a leader is a dynamic process that requires introspection, strategic action, and genuine engagement. By focusing on these four areas, you can establish a leadership brand that resonates with your values, showcases your strengths, builds your desired reputation, and drives you toward your vision.

CHAPTER 8

Trust in Leadership – The Three Circles Approach

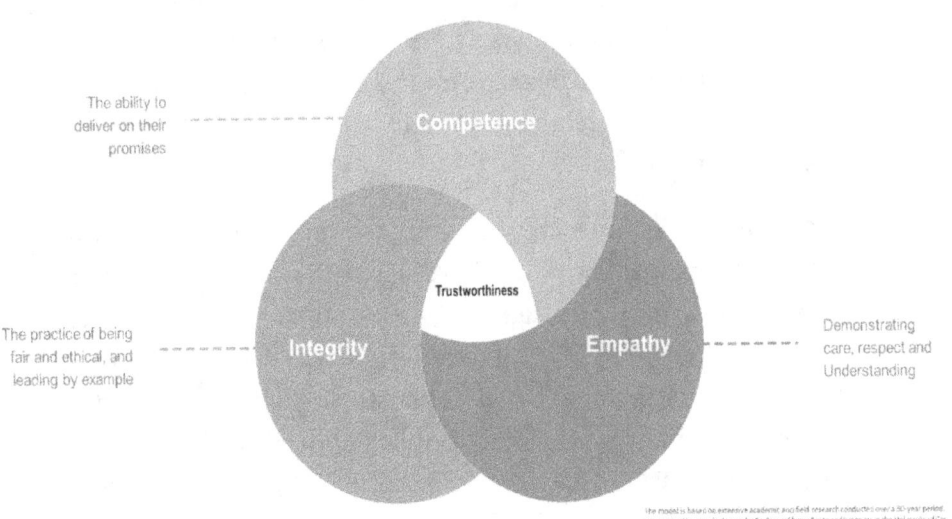

"Without trust we don't truly collaborate; we merely coordinate or, at best, cooperate. It is trust that transforms a group of people into a team."

~ Stephen Covey

In the realm of leadership, trust is not just a nice to have; it's an essential foundation for effective management, employee engagement, and achieving organizational goals. The "Three Circles Approach" to trust in leadership focuses on three critical attributes: Competence, Integrity, and Empathy. Each of these circles represents a core area that leaders must develop and maintain to foster a trusting environment.

Competence

Competence is the first circle, and it refers to the leader's ability to effectively perform their role. It encompasses not only technical skills and knowledge **but also the capacity to make sound decisions, solve problems, and manage resources.** Competence is crucial because it lays the groundwork for a leader's credibility.

Employees are more likely to trust leaders who demonstrate a clear understanding of their roles, show proficiency in their tasks, and exhibit the capability to lead the team towards its goals. This trust is further deepened when leaders are seen actively updating their skills and staying abreast of industry trends and changes, thereby showing commitment to their role and the organization.

Integrity

The second circle, Integrity, is the moral compass of a leader. It involves honesty, ethical behaviour, and consistency in actions and decisions. Leaders with integrity are transparent, keep their promises, and take responsibility for their actions, especially when things go wrong.

Integrity builds trust as it assures team members that their leader operates on a consistent set of ethical principles. This predictability in character gives employees a sense of security and fairness in the workplace, encouraging them to be open, share ideas, and voice concerns without fear of unjust repercussions. Furthermore, leaders who model integrity inspire it in their teams, creating a culture of trustworthiness throughout the organization.

Empathy

The third and equally vital circle is Empathy. This involves the ability to understand and share the feelings of others. Empathetic leaders are attentive to their team members' needs and concerns, and they strive to view situations from others' perspectives.

Empathy in leadership fosters trust by creating a supportive and understanding work environment. When employees feel that their leaders genuinely care about their well-being and professional growth, they are more engaged, motivated, and committed to the organization's success. Empathetic leaders are also better at conflict resolution and building strong, cohesive teams, as they can navigate interpersonal dynamics sensitively and effectively.

Integrating the Three Circles

The true power of the Three Circles Approach lies in the integration of Competence, Integrity, and Empathy. These attributes are interdependent and mutually reinforcing:

- A competent leader without integrity may achieve short-term results but will struggle to earn lasting respect and loyalty from their team.
- A leader with integrity but lacking competence may be admired but not followed, as they fail to guide the team effectively.
- A leader who is empathetic but lacks competence and integrity may be liked but not respected in their professional capacity.

Therefore, for a leader to be fully trustworthy, they must continuously develop and balance all three attributes. This holistic approach to leadership not only builds trust but also drives sustainable success and fosters a positive organizational culture where each member feels valued, understood, and motivated to contribute their best.

In conclusion, the Three Circles Approach to Trust in Leadership offers a comprehensive framework for leaders aspiring to build and maintain a high level of trust within their teams and organizations. By focusing on and harmonizing Competence, Integrity, and Empathy, leaders can create a strong foundation of trust that leads to enhanced team performance, better employee satisfaction, and overall organizational excellence.

CHAPTER 9

Practical Strategies for Enhancing HQ

"Leadership and learning are indispensable to each other."

~ John F. Kennedy

As we journey through the landscape of the Human Quotient (HQ), we have delved into its three integral dimensions - cognitive, behavioural, and interpersonal. We have explored how these dimensions shape a leader's thoughts, actions, and relationships, and how they contribute to effective leadership. Now, it's time to turn our exploration towards the practical side of things. How can we enhance our HQ? What strategies can we employ to develop our cognitive abilities, manage our behaviours, and build strong relationships?

In this chapter, we will provide practical, actionable strategies for enhancing each dimension of HQ. These strategies are grounded in research and have been proven effective in real-world settings. They are designed to help leaders - whether they are seasoned veterans or emerging talents - to enhance their HQ and, in turn, their effectiveness as leaders.

We will explore strategies for enhancing the cognitive dimension of HQ, such as mindful self-reflection and strategic reasoning. We will delve into techniques for managing the behavioural dimension, including emotion regulation, self-management, and mindfulness. And we will discuss ways to build the interpersonal dimension, focusing on relationship-building and effective communication.

By integrating these strategies into your leadership practice, you can enhance your HQ and unlock your full potential as a leader. So, let's dive in and explore these practical strategies for leading with HQ.

Enhancing The Cognitive Dimension

The cognitive dimension of HQ, as we've learned, is about the mental processes that underpin decision-making, problem-solving, and strategic planning. It's about how we think, how we process information, and how we make decisions. To enhance this dimension, we can engage in practices such as mindful self-reflection and strategic reasoning.

Mindful Self-Reflection

Mindful self-reflection is a practice of introspection that involves taking time to reflect on one's thoughts, feelings, and actions, and to learn from one's experiences. It's about stepping back from the hustle and bustle of daily life and taking a moment to look inward, to examine our thoughts and feelings, and to gain a deeper understanding of ourselves.

This practice can help leaders to become more self-aware, to understand their strengths and weaknesses, and to identify areas for growth and development. It can also help leaders to understand their own values and beliefs, and to align their actions with these values.

Practicing mindful self-reflection can be as simple as taking a few minutes each day to sit quietly and reflect on your experiences. You might reflect on a recent decision you made, a challenge you faced, or a conversation you had. The key is to approach this reflection with an open mind and a non-judgmental attitude, to observe your thoughts and feelings without criticism or defensiveness. When reflecting on past experiences, it is best to adopt the mindset of a consultant. As a consultant, you should approach everything as a piece of information without judging whether it is right or wrong, good or bad. The main objective is to identify what was effective and ineffective and use that knowledge to improve future outcomes.

Strategic Reasoning

Strategic reasoning, on the other hand, involves thinking ahead, anticipating future trends and challenges, and developing innovative solutions. It's about looking beyond the immediate situation and considering the bigger picture. It's about thinking creatively and critically and making decisions that are informed by a deep understanding of the current situation and a clear vision of the future. Following are few ways you can enhance your strategic reasoning skills.

Broaden Your Knowledge Base: Engaging with a wide range of disciplines, including economics, psychology, and history, can provide new perspectives and frameworks for understanding complex problems. Diverse knowledge encourages innovative thinking and helps leaders to anticipate trends and potential impacts on their organizations.

Practice Systems Thinking: This involves understanding how different parts of a system interact with each other. Leaders can improve their strategic reasoning by learning to see both the forest and the trees, recognizing patterns, and understanding how changes in one area can affect the whole. Tools like causal loop diagrams can help visualize and explore these relationships.

Develop Foresight: Foresight is the ability to anticipate what might happen in the future and prepare accordingly. Techniques like scenario planning, where leaders imagine various future states and plan how to respond, can improve the ability to anticipate future challenges and opportunities.

Simulation and Visualization of Different "What ifs?": Engaging in simulations or What-if scenario exercises can provide leaders with a safe environment to experiment with different strategies and predict their potential outcomes. These exercises can sharpen decision-making skills, highlight unforeseen challenges, and foster a strategic mindset.

Engage in Strategic Conversations: Regular discussions with a diverse group of people, including those inside and outside the organization, can expose leaders to new ideas and viewpoints. These conversations can challenge assumptions, spark innovation, and provide insights into emerging trends and potential strategies. This is the reason why working with a coach/mentor who is from outside the organisation can be useful.

Seek Feedback and Coaching: Feedback from peers, mentors, or a professional coach can provide valuable insights into a leader's strategic reasoning process, highlighting strengths and identifying areas for improvement. Coaching, in particular, can offer personalized guidance and support for developing specific strategic skills.

Continuous Learning and Adaptability: The business environment is ever-changing, and leaders must continuously learn and adapt. Staying informed about industry trends, technological advancements, and global economic conditions helps leaders make informed strategic decisions.

Mental Models: Developing and utilizing mental models – simplified representations of how things work – can help leaders make better decisions by applying these frameworks to different situations. Familiarity with various models enables leaders to quickly assess situations and determine the most applicable approach.

By focusing on these areas, leaders can significantly enhance their strategic reasoning skills, leading to more effective decision-making and stronger organizational leadership.

Managing The Behavioural Dimension

The behavioural dimension of HQ is about how we act and react in various situations, particularly those that are stressful or challenging. It's about our ability to manage our emotions, to control our behaviours, and to respond to challenges in a thoughtful and constructive manner. To manage this dimension, we can practice emotion regulation, self-management, and mindfulness.

Emotion Regulation

Emotion regulation is an essential component of effective leadership. It encompasses the processes by which individuals influence which emotions they have, when they have them, and how they experience and express these emotions. For leaders, the ability to regulate emotions is crucial as it impacts decision-making, stress management, interpersonal relationships, and overall leadership effectiveness. Below, we expand on the concept and strategies for enhancing emotion regulation:

Understanding Emotion Regulation

1. **Awareness**: The first step in emotion regulation is becoming acutely aware of one's emotional state. This involves recognizing the physical signs of emotions and identifying the feelings as they occur.

2. **Understanding**: Beyond mere recognition, understanding why a certain emotion is being felt is critical. This could involve recognizing the external events or internal thoughts that triggered the emotion.

3. **Choosing a Response**: After recognizing and understanding an emotion, the next step is deciding how to respond. This doesn't necessarily mean suppressing the emotion but rather choosing a response that is constructive and aligned with one's goals.

Importance for Leaders

- **Calm Under Pressure**: Leaders often face high-stakes situations. Emotion regulation allows them to maintain composure, ensuring that stress does not cloud judgment or decision-making.

- **Rational Decision-Making**: By managing emotional responses, leaders can ensure that their decisions are driven by logic and objective analysis rather than by fleeting feelings or undue stress.

- **Conflict Management**: Emotions can escalate conflicts. Leaders skilled in emotion regulation can de-escalate situations, foster understanding, and navigate toward constructive solutions.

Strategies for Enhancing Emotion Regulation

1. **Mindfulness Practices**: Mindfulness involves paying attention to the present moment without judgment. Practices like meditation can increase awareness of emotional states and triggers, creating a space between feeling an emotion and reacting to it.

2. **Cognitive Strategies**:

- **Reframing**: This involves changing the interpretation of a situation to alter its emotional impact. By viewing challenges as opportunities, leaders can maintain a positive outlook and reduce negative emotional responses.
- **Perspective-Taking**: Understanding situations from multiple viewpoints can help leaders empathize with others and reduce personal biases in emotional responses.

3. **Relaxation Techniques**:
    - **Deep Breathing**: Simple yet effective, deep breathing can help calm the mind and body, reducing the intensity of emotional reactions.
    - **Progressive Muscle Relaxation (PMR)**: This technique involves tensing and then slowly relaxing different muscle groups. PMR can reduce physical tension and associated emotional stress.

4. **Physical Exercise**: Regular physical activity can improve mood, reduce stress, and enhance overall emotional well-being, contributing to better emotion regulation.

5. **Building Emotional Vocabulary**: Expanding the vocabulary used to describe emotions can help in accurately identifying and expressing feelings, which is a crucial step in emotion regulation.

6. **Seeking Feedback**: Leaders can benefit from feedback on their emotional responses from trusted colleagues

or mentors. This external perspective can provide insights into how their emotions are perceived and the impact they have on others.

7. **Professional Support**: Sometimes, developing emotion regulation skills can benefit from the guidance of a psychologist or a professional coach, especially for managing more deep-seated emotional patterns or challenges.

Emotion regulation is not about suppressing emotions but rather understanding and managing them in a way that enhances personal well-being and leadership effectiveness. By developing these skills, leaders can navigate the complexities of their roles with greater resilience, empathy, and clarity.

Self-Management

Self-management, on the other hand, involves controlling our behaviours and actions. It's about acting in a way that is consistent with our values and goals, and that contributes to a positive and productive work environment. Self-management can be enhanced by setting clear goals, developing good work habits, and seeking feedback and support when needed.

Mindfulness

Mindfulness is a practice of paying attention in a particular way: on purpose, in the present moment, and non-judgmentally. It involves being fully present in the moment and paying attention to our thoughts, feelings, and sensations without judgment. Mindfulness can help leaders stay calm under pressure, make more mindful decisions, and manage their emotions effectively.

Building the Interpersonal Dimension

The interpersonal dimension of HQ is about the relationships and interactions between leaders and their team members. It's about how leaders connect with others, how they communicate their ideas and feelings, and how they influence and inspire those around them. To build this dimension, we can focus on relationship-building and effective communication.

Relationship-Building

Building strong relationships is a key component of the interpersonal dimension of HQ. It involves developing a deep understanding of others, showing empathy and compassion, and building trust and respect. Leaders with strong interpersonal skills are able to connect with their team members on a personal level, to understand their needs and concerns, and to foster a sense of camaraderie and teamwork.

Building strong relationships requires time, effort, and consistency. It involves regular communication, active listening, and genuine interest in others. It also involves showing appreciation and recognition, providing support and guidance, and being open and transparent.

Effective Communication

Effective communication is another crucial aspect of the interpersonal dimension of HQ. It involves not only speaking clearly and persuasively but also listening actively and empathetically. Effective communication enables leaders to convey their vision and goals, to provide feedback and guidance, and to resolve conflicts constructively.

Effective communication requires a good understanding of communication principles and techniques. It involves being clear and concise, using appropriate body language, and adapting your communication style to suit the situation and the audience. It also involves active listening, which means paying full attention to the speaker, showing empathy, and providing feedback.

Conclusion

Enhancing HQ is a continuous journey of learning and growth. It involves developing a deep understanding of oneself and others, managing one's emotions and behaviours, and building strong and effective relationships. By enhancing their HQ, leaders can become more effective, build stronger teams, and drive success for their organizations. In the next chapter, we will explore case studies of successful leaders who have effectively utilized their HQ to drive success. So, stay tuned as we continue our journey into the world of leading with HQ.

CHAPTER 10

Case Studies of Leading with HQ

Introduction

In our exploration of the Human Quotient (HQ), we have delved into its three integral dimensions - cognitive, behavioural, and interpersonal. We have discussed their significance in leadership and provided practical strategies for enhancing each dimension. Now, it's time to bring theory into practice. In this chapter, we will examine real-world examples of successful leaders who have effectively harnessed their HQ to drive success. These case studies will provide a tangible understanding of how HQ operates in the real world, and how it can be a powerful tool for effective leadership.

These leaders, from various industries and backgrounds, have demonstrated exceptional abilities in one or more dimensions of HQ. They have used their cognitive abilities to innovate and strategize, their behavioural skills to manage themselves and respond effectively to challenges, and their interpersonal skills to build strong relationships and foster positive work environments. Their stories provide valuable insights into how HQ can be applied in practice, and how it can contribute to effective leadership.

Through these case studies, we aim to illustrate the power of HQ in driving success, and to provide inspiration for leaders who are seeking to enhance their own HQ. We will delve into the stories of a visionary leader, a resilient leader, and a people-centric leader, exploring how they have utilized their HQ to overcome challenges, drive innovation, and lead their teams to success. So, let's dive in and explore these inspiring stories of leading with HQ.

Case Study 1: A Visionary Leader

Our first case study focuses on a visionary leader who has harnessed their cognitive HQ to drive innovation and growth in their organization. This leader, whom we'll refer to as Alex, is the CEO of a technology company that has made significant strides in its industry under his leadership.

Alex has demonstrated exceptional strategic reasoning abilities, a key component of the cognitive dimension of HQ. He has shown an uncanny ability to anticipate future trends in the technology industry, and to align his company's strategies with these trends. This forward-thinking approach has allowed his company to stay ahead of the curve and to consistently outperform its competitors.

But Alex's cognitive HQ extends beyond strategic reasoning. He has also shown a commitment to continuous learning and growth, both for himself and for his team. He encourages his team members to pursue learning opportunities, and he himself is always seeking to expand his knowledge and skills. This commitment to learning has fostered a culture of innovation in his company, where new ideas are welcomed and explored.

Furthermore, Alex is not afraid to challenge the status quo. He encourages his team to question existing practices and to seek better ways of doing things. This willingness to challenge and innovate has led to numerous breakthroughs and has contributed to his company's success.

Alex's story is a testament to the power of the cognitive dimension of HQ. His strategic reasoning, commitment to learning, and willingness to challenge the status quo have driven innovation and growth in his company. His leadership exemplifies how enhancing cognitive HQ can lead to effective leadership and organizational success.

Case Study 2: A Resilient Leader

Our second case study focuses on a resilient leader who has effectively managed their behavioural HQ in the face of adversity. This leader, whom we'll refer to as Brenda, is the head of a non-profit organization that faced significant challenges during her tenure.

Brenda's leadership journey was marked by numerous obstacles, including funding cuts and organizational restructuring. However, she demonstrated remarkable resilience in the face of these challenges. Brenda's ability to stay calm under pressure, to manage her emotions effectively, and to respond to challenges in a thoughtful and constructive manner were key to her success.

One of the key aspects of Brenda's behavioural HQ is her ability to regulate her emotions. Despite the stress and uncertainty, Brenda was able to maintain her composure and make rational decisions. She was able to manage her emotions in a way that allowed her to stay focused on her goals and to lead her team effectively.

Brenda also demonstrated strong self-management skills. She was able to control her behaviours and actions, ensuring that they were aligned with her values and goals. Even in the face of adversity, Brenda remained committed to her mission and led her team with integrity and determination.

Furthermore, Brenda practiced mindfulness, which helped her to stay present and focused, even in the midst of challenges. She used mindfulness techniques to manage her stress and to maintain her focus on her goals.

Brenda's story is a powerful example of how the behavioural dimension of HQ can contribute to effective leadership. Her ability to regulate her emotions, manage her behaviours, and practice mindfulness helped her to navigate challenges and lead her organization to success.

Case Study 3: A People-Centric Leader

Our third case study focuses on a people-centric leader who has excelled in the interpersonal dimension of HQ. This leader, whom we'll refer to as Carlos, is the manager of a diverse team within a multinational corporation.

Carlos has demonstrated exceptional abilities in building strong relationships with his team members. Despite the diverse backgrounds and perspectives within his team, Carlos has been able to foster a sense of unity and camaraderie. He has developed a deep understanding of his team members, showing empathy and compassion in his interactions with them. This has helped him to build trust and respect within his team, creating a strong foundation for collaboration and teamwork.

Carlos's effective communication skills have also been key to his success as a leader. He has been able to convey his ideas and expectations clearly and persuasively, ensuring that his team members understand their roles and responsibilities. At the same time, Carlos has shown a commitment to active listening, taking the time to understand his team members' ideas, concerns, and feedback. This two-way communication has fostered a sense of openness and transparency within his team.

Furthermore, Carlos has been able to foster a positive work environment within his team. He has promoted a culture of respect, collaboration, and mutual support, where every team member feels valued and included. This positive work environment has contributed to high levels of engagement and productivity within his team.

Carlos's story is a powerful example of how the interpersonal dimension of HQ can contribute to effective leadership. His ability to build strong relationships, communicate effectively, and foster a positive work environment has helped him to lead his diverse team to success.

Conclusion

These case studies provide valuable insights into how HQ can be applied in practice, and how it can contribute to effective leadership. They illustrate the power of HQ in driving success, and they provide inspiration for leaders who are seeking to enhance their own HQ. In the next chapter, we will provide a summary of the key points discussed in this book, and we will provide some final thoughts on the journey of leading with HQ. So, stay tuned as we conclude our journey into the world of leading with HQ.

CHAPTER 11

Research evidence supporting the principles of HQ

The principles of the Human Quotient (HQ) are supported by a wealth of research from various fields, including psychology, neuroscience, and organizational studies. One of the most notable research programs that support the principles of HQ is Google's Project Aristotle.

Google's Project Aristotle

Project Aristotle, a research initiative by Google, aimed to decode the DNA of successful teams. The project's name was inspired by Aristotle's quote, "The whole is greater than the sum of its parts," reflecting the project's focus on team dynamics rather than individual prowess. Over several years, Google's researchers scrutinized half a century of academic studies and analysed data from more than 180 active teams at Google.

The key finding from Project Aristotle was the concept of "psychological safety," which Harvard Business School professor Amy Edmondson defines as a "shared belief held by members of a team that the team is safe for interpersonal risk-taking." In psychologically safe teams, members feel comfortable taking risks, making mistakes, and bringing their full selves to work, without fear of embarrassment or punishment.

This concept of psychological safety is deeply intertwined with the principles of HQ. It requires proactive communication, where team members actively share information and ideas (cognitive aspect of HQ). It also requires emotional regulation, where team members manage their emotions and reactions, particularly in response to mistakes or failures (behavioural aspect of HQ). Lastly, it requires effective relationship-building, where team members build trust, respect, and mutual understanding (interpersonal aspect of HQ).

Other Supporting Evidence

Beyond Project Aristotle, a wealth of research from various fields supports the principles of HQ. Cognitive psychology and neuroscience have provided insights into the power of proactive thinking and strategic reasoning. Studies have shown that these cognitive abilities are crucial for effective decision-making, problem-solving, and innovation. They enable leaders to anticipate changes, devise effective strategies, and guide their teams towards success.

In the realm of behavioural science, research has underscored the importance of emotional regulation in leadership. Leaders who can manage their emotions and respond effectively to stress are more resilient, make better decisions, and foster healthier team dynamics. They are also better equipped to create an environment where team members feel safe, valued, and motivated.

In terms of the interpersonal dimension of HQ, organizational studies have highlighted the importance of effective relationship-building. Strong relationships, characterized by trust, respect, and mutual understanding, are the bedrock of high-performing teams. Leaders who excel in relationship-building foster better collaboration, higher engagement, and stronger commitment among their team members.

In conclusion, the principles of HQ are not just theoretical concepts but are grounded in extensive research. This body of evidence underscores the importance of HQ in effective leadership and team success and provides a solid foundation for the strategies and practices discussed in this book.

CHAPTER 12

Conclusion and Final Thoughts

As we draw this exploration of the Human Quotient (HQ) to a close, it's time to reflect on the journey we've undertaken. We've traversed the landscape of HQ, delving into its three integral dimensions - cognitive, behavioural, and interpersonal. We've examined the role each dimension plays in effective leadership and explored practical strategies for enhancing each one. We've also brought theory into practice, examining real-world case studies of leaders who have effectively harnessed their HQ to drive success in their respective fields.

This journey has been about more than just understanding a concept. It's been about equipping you, the reader, with the knowledge and tools to enhance your own HQ and, in turn, your effectiveness as a leader. It's been about providing a roadmap for your own journey of leading with HQ.

As we conclude this exploration, we will revisit the key points we've discussed, reflecting on the importance of each dimension of HQ and the strategies for enhancing them. We will also reflect on the journey of leading with HQ, considering what it means to lead with HQ and how it can contribute to effective leadership. So, let's take a moment to reflect on our journey and consider the path ahead.

Revisiting the Human Quotient (HQ)

The Human Quotient, or HQ, is a comprehensive framework for leadership development that is rooted in emerging scientific knowledge. It represents a holistic approach to leadership, encompassing three interwoven components - cognitive, behavioural, and interpersonal. Each of these components plays a crucial role in effective leadership, and together, they form the foundation of HQ.

The cognitive dimension of HQ is about proactive thinking and strategic reasoning. It's about being able to anticipate future trends, make sound decisions, and innovate. The behavioural dimension, on the other hand, is about managing our emotions and behaviours, particularly in stressful or challenging situations. It's about being able to stay calm under pressure, regulate our emotions, and respond to challenges in a thoughtful and constructive manner. The interpersonal dimension is about building strong relationships and communicating effectively. It's about being able to connect with others, understand their needs and concerns, and foster a positive and collaborative work environment.

By enhancing their HQ, leaders can become more proactive, innovative, and effective. They can drive success for themselves and their organizations. They can navigate challenges, seize opportunities, and lead their teams to success. The concept of HQ provides a roadmap for leadership development, offering a comprehensive and practical approach to becoming a more effective leader.

Key Strategies for Enhancing HQ

Enhancing HQ involves developing a deep understanding of oneself and others, managing one's emotions and behaviours, and building strong and effective relationships. We've discussed a range of practical strategies for enhancing each dimension of HQ.

For the cognitive dimension, strategies include mindful self-reflection and strategic reasoning. Mindful self-reflection involves taking time to reflect on one's thoughts, feelings, and actions, and to learn from one's experiences. Strategic reasoning involves thinking ahead, anticipating future trends and challenges, and developing innovative solutions.

For the behavioural dimension, strategies include emotion regulation, self-management, and mindfulness. Emotion regulation involves understanding and managing our emotional responses. Self-management involves controlling our behaviours and actions. Mindfulness involves being fully present in the moment, paying attention to our thoughts, feelings, and sensations without judgment.

For the interpersonal dimension, strategies include relationship-building and effective communication. Relationship-building involves developing a deep understanding of others, showing empathy and compassion, and building trust and respect. Effective communication involves speaking clearly and persuasively, and listening actively and empathetically.

These strategies provide a practical toolkit for enhancing HQ. They offer a roadmap for developing the skills and abilities that underpin effective leadership. By integrating these strategies into their leadership practice, leaders can enhance their HQ and unlock their full potential as leaders.

Leading with HQ in Practice

The case studies we explored provide valuable insights into how HQ can be applied in practice. They illustrate how leaders can use their cognitive abilities to innovate and strategize, their behavioural skills to manage themselves and respond effectively to challenges, and their interpersonal skills to build strong relationships and foster positive work environments. These leaders exemplify the power of HQ in driving success and provide inspiration for others seeking to enhance their own HQ.

From Alex, the visionary leader who harnessed his cognitive HQ to drive innovation and growth, to Brenda, the resilient leader who managed her behavioural HQ in the face of adversity, to Carlos, the people-centric leader who excelled in the interpersonal dimension of HQ, these leaders provide tangible examples of how HQ can be applied in practice. Their stories illustrate the power of HQ in driving success, and they provide inspiration for leaders who are seeking to enhance their own HQ.

As we conclude this exploration, we hope that you have gained a deeper understanding of HQ and its importance in effective leadership. We hope that the strategies and insights provided will serve as a valuable resource in your own leadership journey. Remember, leading with HQ is not a destination, but a journey - a journey of learning, growth, and continuous improvement. So, keep exploring, keep learning, and keep leading with HQ.

CHAPTER 13

Implementing HQ in Your Leadership Journey

Self-Assessment: Understanding Your Current HQ

The journey to enhancing your Human Quotient (HQ) begins with understanding where you currently stand. This initial step involves a thorough self-assessment of your cognitive, behavioural, and interpersonal skills. It's about taking an honest look at yourself, acknowledging your strengths, and identifying areas where improvement is needed.

To assess your cognitive skills, consider your ability to think proactively and strategically. How often do you find yourself reacting to situations rather than anticipating them? How comfortable are you with challenging the status quo and seeking innovative solutions? Reflect on instances where your cognitive skills were put to the test and evaluate your performance.

Next, evaluate your behavioural skills. Consider your ability to regulate your emotions, particularly in stressful or challenging situations. How do you typically respond to stress or adversity? Are you able to maintain your composure and make rational decisions, or do you tend to react impulsively? Reflect on your past behaviours and identify patterns that can provide insights into your behavioural skills.

Finally, assess your interpersonal skills. Consider your ability to build and maintain strong relationships. How effective are you at communicating your ideas and understanding the perspectives of others? Do you foster a positive and collaborative environment, or are there areas of conflict or misunderstanding that need to be addressed? Reflect on your relationships and interactions with others to gain insights into your interpersonal skills.

In addition to self-reflection, consider seeking feedback from others. Colleagues, team members, or mentors can provide valuable insights into your cognitive, behavioural, and interpersonal skills. They can help you to see blind spots that you may have overlooked and provide constructive feedback to guide your HQ enhancement journey.

Understanding your current HQ is a crucial first step in your HQ enhancement journey. It provides a baseline from which you can measure your progress and guides the development of your personal HQ enhancement plan. In the next section, we will discuss how to develop this plan and start your journey towards enhancing your HQ.

Developing a Personal HQ Enhancement Plan

Once you have a clear understanding of your current HQ, the next step is to develop a personal HQ enhancement plan. This plan is your roadmap to enhancing your cognitive, behavioural, and interpersonal skills. It should be tailored to your specific needs and goals, and it should provide a clear path forward.

Start by setting specific, measurable, achievable, relevant, and time-bound (SMART) goals related to enhancing your HQ. For example, if you identified a need to improve your proactive thinking, a goal might be to dedicate 30 minutes each day to strategic planning and forward-thinking activities for the next three months. If you need to improve your emotional regulation, a goal might be to practice mindfulness techniques for 15 minutes each day for the next two months.

Next, outline the strategies you will use to achieve these goals. These strategies should be based on the practical strategies for enhancing HQ that we discussed in previous chapters. For example, to enhance your proactive thinking, you might decide to engage in regular self-reflection, seek out learning opportunities, or challenge existing practices in your organization. To improve your emotional regulation, you might decide to practice mindfulness, engage in regular physical activity, or seek support from a mentor or coach.

Your plan should also include metrics for measuring your progress. These metrics should provide a clear indication of whether you are making progress towards your goals. For example, you might measure your progress in enhancing proactive thinking by tracking the number of new ideas you generate or the number of learning opportunities you engage in. You might measure your progress in improving emotional regulation by tracking your stress levels or the frequency of emotional reactions.

Finally, your plan should include a timeline for achieving your goals. This timeline should provide a clear path forward, with milestones to mark your progress. It should also be flexible enough to allow for adjustments as necessary.

Developing a personal HQ enhancement plan is a crucial step in your HQ journey. It provides a clear roadmap for enhancing your HQ, with specific goals, strategies, metrics, and a timeline. With this plan in place, you are ready to embark on your journey towards enhancing your HQ. In the next section, we will discuss how to implement your HQ enhancement plan.

Implementing Your HQ Enhancement Plan

With a clear plan in place, the next step is to implement your HQ enhancement plan. This involves putting the strategies you've outlined into action. It's about taking intentional steps every day to enhance your cognitive, behavioural, and interpersonal skills. It's about turning your plan into reality.

Start by scheduling time each day to work on your HQ enhancement activities. This could be as simple as setting aside 15 minutes each morning for mindful self-reflection or dedicating an hour each week to strategic planning. Make these activities a priority, just as you would any other important task.

As you implement your plan, be mindful of your progress. Pay attention to changes in your thinking, behaviour, and interactions with others. Are you noticing improvements in your proactive thinking? Are you better able to regulate your emotions in stressful situations? Are your relationships with others improving? These changes, no matter how small, are signs of progress.

Remember to review your progress regularly against the metrics you've set in your plan. This will help you to stay on track and to identify any adjustments that may be needed. If you're not making as much progress as you'd like, don't be discouraged. Enhancing your HQ is a journey, and it's normal to encounter challenges along the way. The key is to stay committed to your plan and to keep moving forward.

Implementing your HQ enhancement plan also involves celebrating your successes. When you achieve a milestone, take the time to acknowledge your achievement. Celebrating your successes, no matter how small, can boost your motivation and keep you engaged in your HQ journey.

Implementing your HQ enhancement plan is a crucial step in your HQ journey. It's about taking action, tracking your progress, and celebrating your successes. With commitment and perseverance, you can enhance your HQ and become a more effective leader. In the next section, we will discuss the importance of seeking support in your HQ journey.

Seeking Support in Your HQ Journey

Enhancing your HQ is not a journey you have to undertake alone. In fact, seeking support from others can be incredibly beneficial. Whether it's a mentor who provides guidance, a coach who offers new perspectives, or a trusted colleague who gives honest feedback, having support can make your HQ journey more effective and enriching.

Mentors can provide valuable insights based on their own experiences. They can guide you through challenges, help you navigate your career, and provide advice on enhancing your HQ. If you don't already have a mentor, consider seeking one out. Look for someone who has experience in your field, who shares your values, and who is willing to invest time in your development.

Coaches, particularly those trained in leadership development or HQ, can provide targeted support to help you enhance your HQ. They can help you understand your current HQ, develop a personalized HQ enhancement plan, and guide you through the process of implementing your plan. They can also provide tools and techniques to help you enhance your cognitive, behavioural, and interpersonal skills.

Trusted colleagues can also provide support in your HQ journey. They can provide feedback on your leadership style, help you understand how others perceive you, and provide insights into your cognitive, behavioural, and interpersonal skills. Consider seeking feedback from a diverse range of colleagues to get a well-rounded view of your HQ.

Remember, seeking support is not a sign of weakness. On the contrary, it's a sign of strength. It shows that you're committed to enhancing your HQ and that you're open to learning and growing. So, don't hesitate to seek support in your HQ journey. It can provide valuable insights, boost your motivation, and help you navigate challenges along the way.

If you would like to work with me personally to improve your or your organisation's leadership, send me an email at anurag@amhwal.com.

In the next section, we will discuss the importance of continuing your HQ journey, even after you've made significant progress.

Continuing Your HQ Journey

Enhancing your HQ is a continuous journey. Even after you've made significant progress, there will always be opportunities for further growth and development. The world of leadership is dynamic and ever-changing, and leaders must continually adapt and evolve to stay effective. This means that enhancing your HQ is not a one-time effort, but a lifelong commitment.

Continuing your HQ journey involves maintaining a growth mindset. This means viewing challenges as opportunities for learning, seeking out new experiences to broaden your perspectives, and being open to feedback and self-improvement. It means recognizing that you can always improve your cognitive, behavioural, and interpersonal skills, no matter how much progress you've already made.

Continuing your HQ journey also involves staying up to date with the latest research and developments in leadership science. This can help you to refine your understanding of HQ and to discover new strategies for enhancing your cognitive, behavioural, and interpersonal skills. Consider attending leadership workshops, reading leadership books, or subscribing to leadership journals to keep your knowledge fresh and relevant.

Finally, continuing your HQ journey involves applying your HQ skills in new and challenging contexts. This can help you to deepen your understanding of HQ and to further enhance your cognitive, behavioural, and interpersonal skills. Whether it's taking on a new leadership role, navigating a complex project, or leading a diverse team, these experiences can provide valuable opportunities for learning and growth.

Continuing your HQ journey is a crucial part of becoming a more effective leader. It's about maintaining a growth mindset, staying informed, and seeking out new challenges. By continuing your HQ journey, you can unlock your full potential as a leader and drive success for your team and your organization.

As we conclude this book, we hope that you feel equipped and inspired to embark on your own journey of leading with HQ. We hope that the strategies and insights provided will serve as a valuable resource in your leadership journey. Remember, leading with HQ is not a destination, but a journey - a journey of learning, growth, and continuous improvement. So, keep exploring, keep learning, and keep leading with HQ.

CHAPTER 14

The Future of Leadership and HQ

As we conclude our exploration of the Human Quotient (HQ), it's important to look ahead to the future of leadership. The landscape of leadership is constantly evolving, shaped by societal changes, technological advancements, and shifting business landscapes. In this final chapter, we will discuss the future of leadership and the role of HQ in this future.

The Evolving Landscape of Leadership

The landscape of leadership is evolving at a rapid pace, driven by a multitude of factors. Technological advancements are reshaping the way we work, communicate, and lead. The rise of digital technologies and artificial intelligence has enabled new forms of collaboration, decision-making, and problem-solving, but it has also introduced new challenges, such as managing remote teams and protecting against cyber threats.

At the same time, societal changes are influencing the expectations and demands placed on leaders. The increasing diversity of the workforce, for example, requires leaders to be more inclusive and culturally competent. The growing awareness of social and environmental issues is pushing leaders to prioritize sustainability and corporate social responsibility. The ongoing effects of the global pandemic are forcing leaders to navigate uncertainty, adapt quickly to change, and ensure the well-being of their teams.

The business landscape is also changing, with new business models emerging, competitive dynamics shifting, and the pace of change accelerating. In this environment, leaders need to be more agile, innovative, and customer-focused. They need to be able to anticipate and respond to changes in the market, to drive continuous innovation, and to create value for a wide range of stakeholders.

In this rapidly evolving landscape, the skills and abilities encapsulated in HQ - proactive thinking, emotional regulation, and effective relationship-building - are becoming increasingly important. Leaders need to be able to think proactively to anticipate and respond to changes, to regulate their emotions to stay resilient in the face of challenges, and to build strong relationships to foster collaboration and inclusion.

The Role of HQ in the Future of Leadership

As the landscape of leadership continues to evolve, the role of the Human Quotient (HQ) in effective leadership is set to become even more significant. The cognitive, behavioural, and interpersonal dimensions of HQ are not just desirable traits but are becoming essential competencies for leaders in the future.

The cognitive dimension of HQ, which encompasses proactive thinking and strategic reasoning, will be crucial in navigating the complexities of the future business environment. Leaders will need to anticipate changes, make sound decisions amidst uncertainty, and drive innovation to stay competitive. They will need to challenge the status quo, embrace new technologies, and develop forward-thinking business strategies.

The behavioural dimension of HQ, which involves emotional regulation and self-management, will be key in managing the increasing pressures and challenges that leaders face. The ability to stay calm under pressure, to respond rather than react to stressful situations, and to maintain a positive and resilient mindset will be critical. Leaders will need to model these behaviours to foster a resilient and positive organizational culture.

The interpersonal dimension of HQ, which involves relationship-building and effective communication, will be essential in leading diverse and dispersed teams. Leaders will need to foster a culture of inclusion, to communicate effectively across different mediums, and to build strong relationships based on trust and respect. They will need to leverage these relationships to drive collaboration, innovation, and performance.

In this future landscape, enhancing HQ will be a key strategy for leaders to navigate the challenges and seize the opportunities that lie ahead. Leaders who can enhance their HQ will be well-equipped to lead their teams and organizations to success in this changing landscape. In the next section, we will discuss how you can prepare for the future by enhancing your HQ.

Conclusion: The Journey Continues

As we conclude our exploration of the Human Quotient (HQ), it's important to remember that this is not the end of your journey, but rather the beginning. The journey to enhancing your HQ is a lifelong endeavour, one that requires continuous learning, growth, and adaptation.

The world of leadership is dynamic and ever-changing. As societal trends evolve, as technology advances, and as the business landscape shifts, new challenges and opportunities will continually arise. In this context, the ability to think proactively, to regulate emotions effectively, and to build strong relationships will be more important than ever. These are the skills that will equip you to navigate the complexities of the future, to lead with confidence and effectiveness, and to drive success for your team and your organization.

As you continue your journey, remember that enhancing your HQ is not a solitary endeavour. Seek support from mentors, coaches, and colleagues. Engage in continuous learning, whether through formal education, professional development opportunities, or self-directed learning. Seek out new experiences and challenges that will stretch your skills and push you out of your comfort zone.

And finally, remember to celebrate your successes along the way. Each step you take towards enhancing your HQ, no matter how small, is a step towards becoming a more effective leader. Celebrate these achievements and use them as motivation to continue your journey.

As we conclude this book, I hope that you feel equipped and inspired to continue your journey of leading with HQ. We hope that the strategies and insights provided will serve as a valuable resource in your leadership journey. Remember, leading with HQ is not a destination, but a journey - a journey of learning, growth, and continuous improvement. So, keep exploring, keep learning, and keep leading with HQ. The future of leadership is in your hands.

BONUS

CHAPTERS

CHAPTER 15

Introducing The Human Intelligence Model©

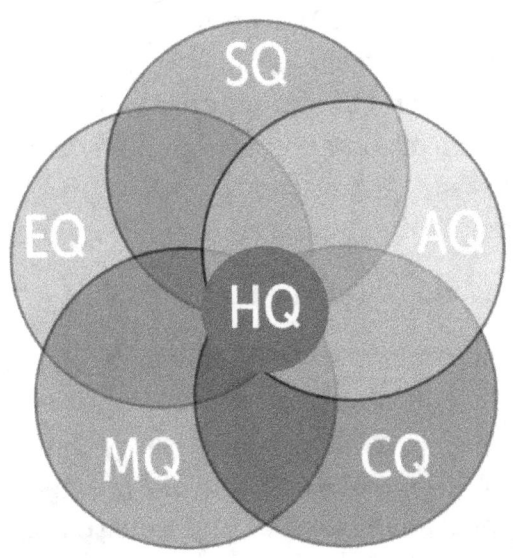

In the rapidly evolving landscape of the 21st century, we have transitioned from the Industrial Age to the Information Age, then to the Conceptual Age, and now to the AI Age. This swift evolution has brought about profound changes in the way we live, work, and interact. However, our education system, largely rooted in the paradigms of the Industrial Age, has struggled to keep pace with these changes. A paradigm shift is required for success in this new era, and traditional measures of intelligence, such as Intelligence Quotient (IQ), may no longer suffice.

In this new context, five new determinants of individual or organizational success have emerged. These determinants form the Human Intelligence Model, a comprehensive framework that recognizes the multifaceted nature of intelligence required to lead in the modern world.

EQ - Emotional Quotient

Emotional Quotient (EQ) refers to a person's ability to perceive, understand, and manage their own emotions, as well as recognize and empathize with the emotions of others. In a world where collaboration and empathy are key, EQ enables individuals and organizations to build strong relationships, foster teamwork, and create a positive organizational culture.

MQ - Motivational Quotient

Motivational Quotient (MQ) represents an individual's ability to motivate and drive themselves and others to pursue and achieve desired goals. In an increasingly competitive and goal-driven world, MQ is essential for maintaining focus, perseverance, and resilience, and for inspiring others to strive for excellence.

CQ - Cultural Quotient

Cultural Quotient (CQ) is the ability to navigate and adapt to diverse cultural contexts with understanding, sensitivity, and effectiveness. As globalization continues to bring diverse cultures into closer contact, CQ is vital for cross-cultural communication, collaboration, and innovation.

SQ - Social Quotient

Social Quotient (SQ) refers to a person's ability to understand and navigate social interactions, build and maintain relationships, and effectively communicate and collaborate with others. In an interconnected world, SQ is essential for networking, influencing, and building strong communities.

AQ - Adversity Quotient

Adversity Quotient (AQ) represents an individual's capacity to face and overcome challenges, bounce back from setbacks, and adapt effectively in the face of adversity. In a rapidly changing world filled with uncertainty, AQ is crucial for resilience, flexibility, and the ability to thrive in the face of challenges.

The Human Intelligence Model introduces a new paradigm for understanding intelligence in the AI Age. It recognizes that success in the modern world requires a multifaceted approach to intelligence, encompassing not just cognitive abilities but also emotional, motivational, cultural, social, and adversity intelligence. By embracing this comprehensive model, individuals and organizations can equip themselves with the tools and insights needed to thrive in a rapidly changing world.

At AMHWAL Academy we provide online trainings to help you develop each of the facets of the Human Intelligence Model. Get in touch by sending an email to info@amhwal.com.

CHAPTER 16

Leadability – The Foundation of Effective Leadership

Leadership Skill = Knowledge x Leadability

In the complex world of leadership, where knowing what to do does not equate doing it, and deep understanding influences what comes next, the idea of Leadability becomes very important. It invites leaders to go above and beyond the usual. This chapter takes another look at Leadability, seeing it not just as a skill but as a combination of being physically, mentally, and spiritually prepared for the challenges leaders face day to day. Here, we redefine the leadership equation: Leadership Skill = Knowledge x Leadability, proposing that Leadability itself is grounded in a holistic approach to fitness.

Unpacking the Enigma of Inaction

The paradox of leadership often lies in the gap between knowledge and action. Leaders are typically well-versed in what needs to be done but falter in the execution. This gap, this chasm, stems from a deficiency not of knowledge, but of Leadability - the very essence of leadership ability. It's an ability that encompasses far more than strategic thinking or decision-making prowess; it's rooted in the comprehensive fitness of the leader.

Leadability: A Holistic Approach

Leadability transcends the conventional understanding of leadership abilities. It is not just about leading others but also about leading oneself. The journey to enhancing Leadability begins with acknowledging the triad of leadership fitness: physical, mental, and spiritual. Each element plays a crucial role in shaping a leader who can navigate complexities with grace and efficacy.

Physical Fitness: The Foundation of Vitality

Physical fitness is the bedrock of Leadability. It's not merely about endurance or strength but about cultivating a body that can sustain the demands of leadership. A leader in good physical health radiates energy and vitality, inspiring confidence and resilience in their teams. Regular exercise, balanced nutrition, and adequate rest are not luxuries but necessities for the effective leader.

Mental Fitness: The Realm of Clarity and Creativity

Mental fitness is the ability to maintain clarity, focus, and critical thinking under pressure. It involves cultivating a mindset that embraces challenges as opportunities for growth. Mental fitness also encompasses emotional intelligence, the capacity to understand and manage emotions in oneself and in others. A mentally fit leader navigates stressful situations with composure, making decisions with a clear and creative mind.

Spiritual Fitness: The Compass of Purpose

Spiritual fitness is perhaps the most abstract yet profound aspect of Leadability. It is about aligning with one's core values and purpose, fostering a sense of connectedness to something greater than oneself. This spiritual grounding provides a reservoir of strength and resilience, guiding leaders through ethical dilemmas and enabling them to inspire and uplift others. It's not necessarily religious but deeply personal, reflecting a commitment to authenticity and ethical leadership.

Cultivating Leadability: Strategies for Holistic Fitness

Building Leadability requires intentional effort across the triad of leadership fitness. Here are strategies to cultivate each aspect:

1. **Enhance Physical Fitness:** Commit to regular physical activity tailored to your preferences and needs. Prioritize sleep and nutrition to fuel your body and mind for the demands of leadership.

2. **Strengthen Mental Fitness:** Engage in continuous learning and critical thinking exercises. Practice mindfulness and stress-reduction techniques to enhance emotional intelligence and resilience.

3. **Deepen Spiritual Fitness:** Spend time in reflection to clarify your values and purpose. Engage in practices that nurture your spiritual well-being, whether through

meditation, nature walks, or journaling, to strengthen your ethical compass.

In essence, Leadability is the manifestation of a leader's comprehensive fitness. It transforms theoretical knowledge into practical wisdom and potential into impactful action. By embracing a holistic approach to fitness, leaders can bridge the gap between knowing and doing, guiding their teams toward shared visions with vitality, clarity, and purpose. The journey to enhancing Leadability is ongoing, a path of continuous growth and self-discovery. Embrace this journey with commitment and curiosity, for it is through the cultivation of physical, mental, and spiritual fitness that the true essence of leadership is revealed.

CHAPTER 17

Psychological Safety: The Essential Environment for Thriving Teams

"Without Psychological Safety, diversity of any kind is only as good as some numbers on the board".

~ **Anurag Rai**

In today's rapidly evolving work environments, creating a culture where employees feel empowered to speak up, take risks, and learn from mistakes is more crucial than ever. Psychological safety is the foundation of such a culture, and it's becoming increasingly recognized as a vital component for individual and organizational success. Let's delve into this powerful concept.

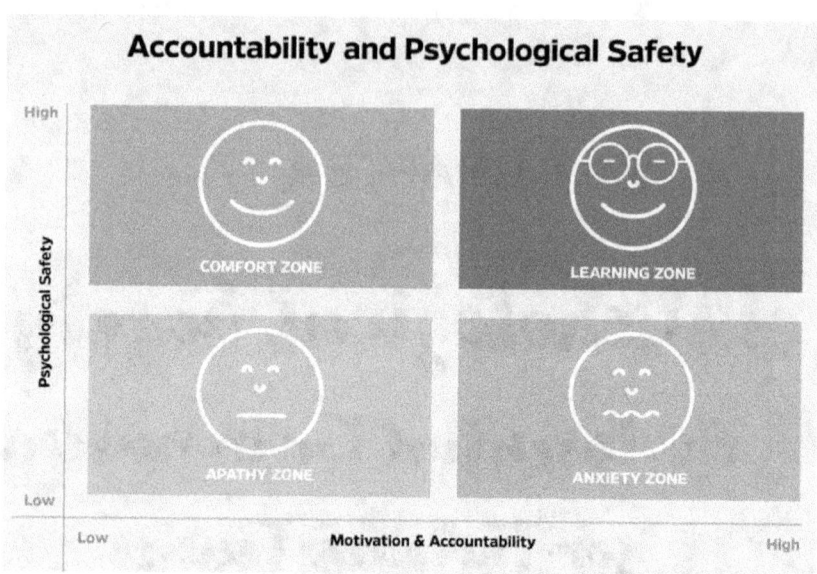

Amy Edmondson Psychological Safety Model

What is Psychological Safety?

Pioneered by Harvard Business School professor Amy Edmondson, psychological safety is defined as "a shared belief held by members of a team that the team is safe for interpersonal risk-taking." In simpler terms, it's the feeling that one can voice opinions, share concerns, ask questions, or even admit errors without fear of embarrassment, retaliation, or negative consequences.

Importance of Psychological Safety

Psychological safety plays a multifaceted role in the workplace. Here's why it matters:

- **Enhanced Performance:** Teams with a high degree of psychological safety experience greater collaboration, leading to higher levels of productivity and innovation.

- **Improved Learning:** Psychologically safe environments foster vulnerability and encourage employees to admit mistakes, facilitating continuous learning and knowledge-sharing.

- **Elevated Engagement and Job Satisfaction:** Employees who feel safe and supported are more likely to be engaged, satisfied, and less likely to face burnout.

- **Boost in Creativity and Innovation:** When individuals aren't afraid to propose unconventional ideas or challenge the status quo, unprecedented breakthroughs become possible.

How the Concept Evolved

While Edmondson's research brought psychological safety into mainstream focus, the concept has its roots in earlier studies on group dynamics and organizational learning. Management thinkers like Peter Senge and Chris Argyris had already emphasized the importance of open communication and constructive feedback for team success. Edmondson's unique contribution was in coining the term "psychological safety" and conducting extensive studies that proved its direct impact on team performance.

The 4 Stages of Psychological Safety

Psychological safety isn't a binary on/off switch. It's a developmental journey that teams progress through. Here's a breakdown of the 4 stages outlined by Timothy R. Clark, along with a visual representation:

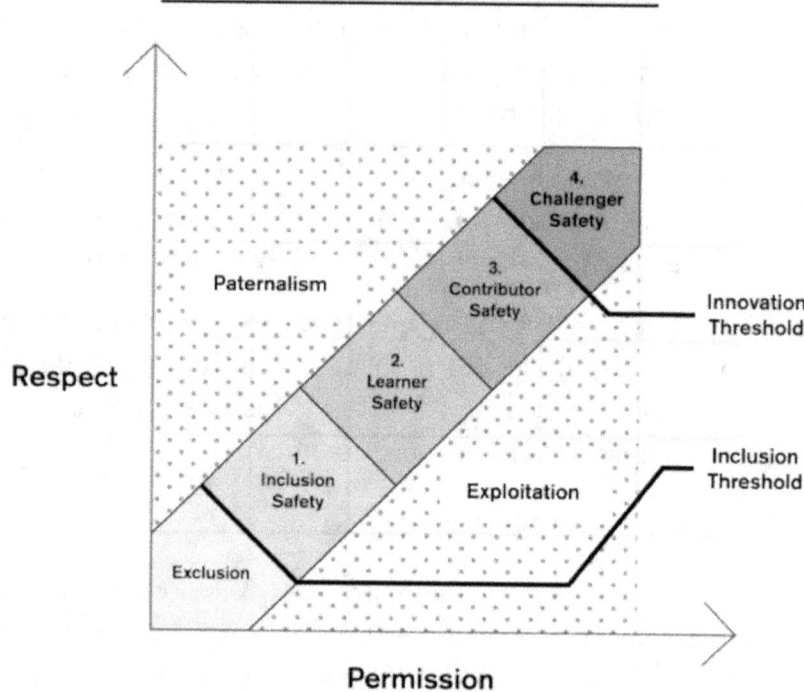

Tim Clark's "Four Stages of Psychological Safety" Model.
From "The Four Stages of Psychological Safety"

1. **Inclusion Safety (Feeling Safe to Belong):** This is the foundation. Team members feel welcome, respected, and valued. They are comfortable being themselves and participating without fear of exclusion.

2. **Learner Safety (Feeling Safe to Learn):** Here, the focus is on psychological safety for experimentation and growth. Team

members feel empowered to ask questions, admit mistakes, and take calculated risks without repercussions. This stage fosters a growth mindset and continuous learning.

3. **Contributor Safety (Feeling Safe to Contribute):** At this stage, team members feel comfortable sharing their ideas and expertise. They believe their contributions will be heard and valued, leading to increased collaboration and innovation.

4. **Challenger Safety (Feeling Safe to Challenge the Status Quo):** This is the most advanced stage. Team members feel confident questioning assumptions, offering dissenting opinions, and proposing alternative approaches, even to senior leaders. This fosters healthy debate and leads to more well-rounded decisions.

Progression Through the Stages

It's important to note that this progression isn't always linear. Teams may revisit earlier stages or move through them at different paces. The key is to be mindful of where your team stands and take steps to foster a psychologically safe environment at all levels.

Two ways to build both respect and permission, specifically tailored to fostering psychological safety:

Building Respect

1. **Demonstrate Genuine Empathy:** Take the time to actively understand your team members' perspectives, challenges, and needs. Show that you care about their

well-being and value their unique experiences. This builds trust and makes them feel seen as individuals.

2. **Practice Inclusive Decision-Making:** Even if you're the ultimate decision-maker, solicit input and ideas from your team members before finalizing choices. Explain the reasoning behind your decisions, showing that their contributions were considered even if the final direction is different.

Building Permission

1. **Provide Autonomy and Trust:** Offer your team members room to make their own decisions within defined parameters. Trust their expertise and judgment, and give them the flexibility to find solutions that align with overarching goals. This sense of ownership encourages engagement.

2. **Celebrate Calculated Risk-Taking:** Make it clear that intelligent risks are welcome. Support team members who want to try new approaches or experiment with ideas, even if there's a chance of failure. Emphasize that the journey towards innovation often involves learning from what doesn't work.

Key Point: Respect and permission go hand-in-hand in building psychological safety. Respecting individuals allows them to feel safe, while offering permission empowers them to actively contribute and feel a sense of agency within the team.

How Leaders Can Create Psychological Safety in the Workplace

- **Embrace Vulnerability:** As a leader, admit your own mistakes and limitations. This powerful gesture signals to your team that it's acceptable to be imperfect.

- **Frame Work as a Learning Process:** Emphasize that mistakes and setbacks are essential steps on the path to improvement.

- **Invite Participation:** Actively solicit input from all levels of your team, ensuring everyone feels heard and valued.

- **Celebrate Curiosity:** Encourage a culture of questioning and asking for help.

- **Focus on Solutions, Not Blame:** When issues arise, shift the emphasis from who's responsible to how the problem can be collectively solved.

Common Misconceptions about Psychological Safety

"Psychological safety is not relaxing your standards, feeling comfortable, being nice and agreeable, or giving unconditional praise."

~ Adam Grant

- **Psychological Safety = "Being Nice"** Although kindness is essential, psychological safety goes beyond simple congeniality. It's about fostering an environment where constructive criticism and difficult conversations are welcome.

- **Psychological Safety = Lack of Accountability** Quite the opposite. Psychological safety encourages accountability by making it easier for team members to raise concerns and collaborate effectively.

How to Know if Your Team Has It?

Ask yourself these questions:

- Do team members feel comfortable challenging ideas, even if they come from senior management?
- Are people willing to speak openly about both successes and failures?
- Is there a healthy focus on continuous learning?
- Are differing opinions respected and thoughtfully considered?

In Conclusion Psychological safety is not a simple matter of feel-good sentiment; it's a strategic investment in a resilient, high-performing team. As a leader, actively cultivating this environment allows your team to unlock their full potential and thrive in a complex and ever-evolving work landscape.

CHAPTER 18

What is your Leadership Style?

Leadership style refers to the manner and approach of providing direction, implementing plans, and motivating people. It encompasses how a leader communicates, makes decisions, and handles various situations. Leadership styles can vary widely depending on factors such as the leader's personality, the nature of the organization, the goals being pursued, and the individuals being led. Each leadership style has its strengths and weaknesses, and effective leaders often adapt their approach based on the circumstances they face.

Why You Should Know Your Leadership Style

Understanding your leadership style is crucial for several reasons:

1. **Self-awareness**: Knowing your leadership style allows you to understand your strengths and areas for

improvement as a leader. It enables you to leverage your natural tendencies while also recognizing situations where a different approach may be more effective.

2. **Communication**: Awareness of your leadership style helps you communicate your expectations and preferences to your team members clearly. It fosters transparency and trust, leading to better collaboration and alignment towards common goals.

3. **Team Dynamics**: Different team members may respond better to certain leadership styles than others. Understanding your style enables you to tailor your approach to the needs and preferences of individual team members, thereby maximizing team effectiveness.

4. **Conflict Resolution**: Recognizing your leadership style can help you identify potential sources of conflict within your team and address them proactively. It allows you to adapt your leadership approach to defuse tension and promote harmony among team members.

The Importance of Switching Between Different Leadership Styles

While having a preferred leadership style is valuable, effective leaders recognize the importance of flexibility and adaptability. The ability to switch between different leadership styles is crucial for navigating diverse challenges and maximizing team performance. Here's why:

1. **Matching the Situation**: No single leadership style is universally effective. Different situations call for different approaches. For example, a crisis may require a more directive leadership style to provide clarity and decisiveness, whereas a creative brainstorming session may benefit from a more participative approach that encourages input from team members.

2. **Flexibility**: Organizations and teams are dynamic entities that evolve over time. What works well in one context may not be as effective in another. Leaders who can adapt their style to changing circumstances are better equipped to address emerging challenges and seize new opportunities.

3. **Empowering Team Members**: Switching between leadership styles enables leaders to empower their team members by giving them opportunities to take on different roles and responsibilities. By delegating authority and fostering autonomy, leaders can develop the skills and confidence of their team members, ultimately strengthening the overall capacity of the team.

4. **Resilience and Innovation**: Diversity of thought and approach is essential for fostering innovation and resilience within organizations. By embracing a range of leadership styles, leaders encourage creative thinking and experimentation, driving continuous improvement and adaptability in the face of uncertainty.

Understanding your leadership style, its implications, and the ability to switch between different styles are fundamental aspects of effective leadership. By cultivating self-awareness, flexibility, and a willingness to adapt, leaders can inspire their teams, navigate complex challenges, and achieve sustainable success in today's dynamic and rapidly changing world.

The following pages include a Leadership Style Quiz that you can use to gain insights on your own leadership style. I hope you find it easy to use, enjoyable and insightful.

Disclaimer for Leadership Style Quiz

This Leadership Style Quiz is designed for educational and developmental purposes only. It aims to provide insights into your preferred leadership styles and approaches based on your responses to the given scenarios. Please note the following important points before you begin:

1. **Subjectivity:** The outcomes of this quiz reflect subjective interpretations of leadership behaviours and tendencies. They are intended to prompt reflection and discussion rather than serve as definitive assessments of your leadership capabilities.

2. **Context Sensitivity:** Effective leadership is highly context dependent. Your most effective leadership style can vary depending on the specific situation, team dynamics, organizational culture, and other external factors. This quiz does not account for all possible variables and nuances.

3. **Not a Diagnostic Tool:** This quiz is not designed to diagnose personality traits or psychological states. It should not be used as the sole basis for making significant decisions regarding career development, employment, or professional relationships.

4. **Use as a Development Tool:** We encourage you to use the results as a starting point for personal development and learning. Consider discussing your results with a mentor, coach, or peers to gain deeper insights and develop strategies for enhancing your leadership effectiveness.

By participating in this quiz, you acknowledge and agree to the terms outlined in this disclaimer. The goal is to offer you an insight for growth and learning, helping you to explore and expand your leadership potential.

Leadership Style Quiz

Instructions: For each question, select the option that best describes your usual approach or reaction in the given scenario. Total number of Questions – 20.

Decision-Making

1. When a critical decision needs to be made quickly:

    - A) I make the decision based on my experience and judgment.

    - B) I gather my team's opinions before making the final decision.

    - C) I encourage innovative solutions and decide based on the best idea.

    - D) I use rewards or consequences to guide the decision-making process.

    - E) I consider what will best serve my team's needs and growth.

    - F) I provide guidelines but ultimately leave the decision to my team.

    - G) My approach depends on the team's skill level and the urgency of the situation.

Communication

2. In communicating expectations to my team:

    - A) I clearly state what needs to be done and expect compliance.

- B) I facilitate a discussion on expectations and reach a consensus.
- C) I inspire them with a vision of what we are trying to achieve together.
- D) I set specific goals and link them to rewards or feedback.
- E) I focus on how our goals align with their personal growth and development.
- F) I offer guidance if asked but generally trust them to know what is expected.
- G) My communication style adapts to the maturity and needs of the team members.

Feedback

3. When providing feedback:
   - A) I'm direct and focus on what needs to change.
   - B) I encourage a two-way conversation and consider their perspective.
   - C) I emphasize how their efforts contribute to the bigger picture and inspire improvement.
   - D) I link feedback to specific rewards or improvements in performance.
   - E) I ensure the feedback serves their development and reinforces their value to the team.

- F) I prefer to let them self-assess unless they seek my input.
- G) The way I give feedback varies with the situation and the individual's needs.

Motivation

4. To motivate my team:
   - A) I set clear goals and monitor progress closely.
   - B) I build consensus and foster a sense of shared purpose.
   - C) I challenge them to surpass their previous achievements and innovate.
   - D) I offer incentives for reaching targets and consequences for falling short.
   - E) I focus on serving their needs and removing obstacles to their success.
   - F) I give them autonomy and trust in their ability to self-motivate.
   - G) I adapt my motivational strategies based on the task and team dynamics.

Problem-Solving

5. When confronted with a team issue:
   - A) I analyse the situation and dictate a solution.
   - B) We discuss the issue as a team and decide on the solution together.

- C) I encourage creative thinking to overcome the challenge in a new way.
- D) I focus on what will quickly fix the issue with minimal disruption.
- E) I listen to everyone's needs and concerns before suggesting a solution.
- F) I allow the team to handle it unless it escalates beyond their control.
- G) My approach is flexible, considering the complexity of the issue and team expertise.

Team Development

6. Regarding team development:
   - A) I ensure they have the necessary skills to follow directives efficiently.
   - B) I foster a learning environment where everyone contributes to each other's growth.
   - C) I push them to expand their capabilities and think outside the box.
   - D) I implement structured training that aligns with organizational objectives.
   - E) I prioritize their personal and professional development in our activities.
   - F) I support their initiatives for self-improvement but don't actively intervene.

- G) I tailor development opportunities to the team's current stage and future needs.

Vision Setting

7. When setting a vision for my team, I:

    - A) Define the vision myself and instruct the team on how to achieve it.
    - B) Involve the team in creating the vision to ensure it reflects our collective goals.
    - C) Paint a compelling picture of the future to inspire and motivate the team towards it.
    - D) Align the vision with specific targets and rewards for achieving those milestones.
    - E) Ensure the vision serves both the organization's goals and the personal growth of team members.
    - F) Provide a broad vision but leave the details to the team to encourage ownership.
    - G) Adapt the vision based on the team's feedback and the changing environment.

Influence

8. To influence others, I:

    - A) Rely on my authority and the clarity of my directives.
    - B) Build consensus and foster mutual respect within the team.

- C) Use inspirational messages and lead by example to drive action.
- D) Set clear expectations and link them to rewards or consequences.
- E) Prioritize relationships and show genuine concern for team members.
- F) Encourage independence and provide support only when necessary.
- G) Use a combination of strategies based on what the situation demands.

Adaptability

9. In adapting to change, I:
    - A) Quickly assess the situation and determine a course of action.
    - B) Involve the team in finding flexible solutions to new challenges.
    - C) Emphasize the opportunities that change brings and inspire the team to adapt.
    - D) Adjust plans and goals based on the change, ensuring clear communication of new targets.
    - E) Focus on how change affects team members and help them navigate through it.
    - F) Trust the team's ability to adapt independently, providing guidance as needed.

- G) Evaluate the situation and team's capability, adapting my leadership style accordingly.

Team Diversity

10. When managing a diverse team, I:
    - A) Ensure all team members understand and adhere to common goals and standards.
    - B) Promote an inclusive environment where different perspectives are valued.
    - C) Leverage diversity to foster creativity and innovation within the team.
    - D) Recognize and reward contributions that highlight the strength of our diversity.
    - E) Prioritize understanding and addressing the unique needs of each team member.
    - F) Provide equal opportunities for all team members to contribute and develop.
    - G) Adapt my approach to ensure it resonates with the diverse backgrounds within my team.

Strategic Execution

11. In executing a strategy, I:
    - A) Plan meticulously and ensure that each team member knows their specific roles.
    - B) Facilitate collaboration to ensure that the strategy is robust and achievable.

- C) Keep the team focused on our long-term goals, even when faced with obstacles.
- D) Use performance metrics to guide the team and adjust tactics as needed.
- E) Support the team's efforts by aligning resources and removing barriers to success.
- F) Allow the team flexibility in how they achieve the strategy's objectives.
- G) Continuously assess the team's progress and the strategy's relevance, making adjustments as necessary.

Team Morale

12. To boost team morale, I:
    - A) Implement rewards and recognize achievements to motivate the team.
    - B) Hold team-building activities and encourage open communication.
    - C) Share inspiring stories and set ambitious goals to energize the team.
    - D) Offer incentives for team milestones to encourage progress.
    - E) Ensure that the work environment caters to team members' well-being and personal growth.

- F) Give the team autonomy, believing that trust in their abilities boosts morale.
- G) Adapt my approach based on the team's current morale and specific needs.

Learning and Development

13. In promoting learning and development within the team, I:

    - A) Direct team members towards specific training programs that enhance operational efficiency.
    - B) Create opportunities for shared learning and mentorship among team members.
    - C) Encourage exploration of new ideas and learning from failures as growth opportunities.
    - D) Link learning objectives to performance metrics and rewards.
    - E) Focus on each team member's career path and align opportunities with their aspirations.
    - F) Provide resources for self-directed learning and support their initiatives.
    - G) Consider individual and team development needs, offering flexible learning options.

Resilience

14. To build resilience in the team, I:

- A) Set clear expectations and create a structured environment to navigate challenges.

- B) Promote a supportive culture where team members feel safe sharing concerns and challenges.

- C) Inspire with a vision that helps the team see beyond immediate setbacks.

- D) Implement a feedback loop that includes constructive criticism and recognition of efforts.

- E) Prioritize emotional intelligence and empathy to understand and address team concerns.

- F) Encourage autonomy and decision-making to strengthen their problem-solving skills.

- G) Adapt leadership strategies based on the team's response to stress and failure.

Ethical Leadership

15. My approach to ethical leadership involves:

    - A) Setting clear rules and consequences to ensure compliance with ethical standards.

    - B) Facilitating discussions on ethics and values, encouraging team input on ethical dilemmas.

    - C) Leading by example and demonstrating integrity in all decisions and actions.

- D) Aligning rewards with ethical behaviour and making ethics a part of performance evaluations.

- E) Putting the team's and stakeholders' interests first and making transparency a priority.

- F) Providing guidelines but ultimately trusting the team to make ethical decisions.

- G) Evaluating the context of each situation and considering the team's values in ethical decision-making.

Personal Growth

16. Regarding my own leadership development, I:

    - A) Focus on strengthening my decision-making and directive capabilities.

    - B) Seek feedback from my team and peers to understand different perspectives.

    - C) Continuously look for inspiration and innovative ideas to improve my leadership.

    - D) Monitor my performance through specific metrics and seek to improve them.

    - E) Reflect on my leadership impact and focus on becoming a more empathetic leader.

    - F) Learn from my experiences and maintain flexibility in my leadership approach.

- G) Assess the effectiveness of my leadership style in different situations and adjust as needed.

Conflict Resolution

17. When dealing with conflict within the team, I:

    - A) Quickly step in to make decisions to resolve the issue.
    - B) Facilitate a meeting where everyone involved can voice their concerns and work towards a solution.
    - C) Encourage the team to view the conflict as a growth opportunity and to find an innovative resolution.
    - D) Focus on mediating the conflict to maintain productivity and set specific outcomes to be achieved.
    - E) Prioritize understanding everyone's needs and guiding them towards a resolution that serves the collective well-being.
    - F) Monitor the situation but allow the team to resolve their conflicts independently.
    - G) My strategy is tailored to the nature of the conflict and the individuals involved.

Strategic Planning

18. In strategic planning and setting long-term goals, I:

- A) Define the strategy and goals based on the organization's needs and expect the team to align.

- B) We collaboratively set strategic goals, ensuring everyone's perspectives are considered.

- C) Guide the team towards setting ambitious goals that push the boundaries of what's possible.

- D) Establish clear, measurable goals and outline the rewards for achieving them.

- E) Ensure the strategy aligns with the team's growth and our ability to serve our stakeholders effectively.

- F) Provide a broad vision but leave the specifics of the strategic plan to the team's discretion.

- G) Adapt our strategic planning process to the team's current capabilities and the external environment.

Adaptability

19. When the team faces unexpected challenges or changes, I:

    - A) Take charge to ensure stability and direct the team on how to adapt.

    - B) Discuss the situation as a team and collectively decide on the best course of action.

- C) Encourage the team to see the challenge as an opportunity for innovation and growth.
- D) Focus on maintaining operational efficiency and adjust targets as necessary.
- E) Be attentive to the team's concerns and support them in navigating the change.
- F) Trust the team to manage their adjustments and offer support when needed.
- G) My response varies, depending on the nature of the challenge and the team's dynamics.

Empowerment

20. When it comes to empowering the team, I:
    - A) Give clear directions to ensure they know what is expected and can execute tasks efficiently.
    - B) Involve them in decision-making processes, enhancing their sense of ownership and responsibility.
    - C) Challenge them to take on new responsibilities and think creatively about solutions.
    - D) Link empowerment to performance metrics, rewarding those who take initiative.
    - E) Focus on understanding their aspirations and provide opportunities for them to lead.

- F) Provide the resources they need and trust them to make their own decisions.

- G) Tailor my approach to each team member's readiness and willingness to take on more responsibility.

Scoring Guide:

- Mostly A's: Autocratic Leadership
- Mostly B's: Democratic Leadership
- Mostly C's: Transformational Leadership
- Mostly D's: Transactional Leadership
- Mostly E's: Servant Leadership
- Mostly F's: Laissez-faire Leadership
- Mostly G's: Situational Leadership

This quiz offers a nuanced view, allowing respondents to identify with aspects of multiple leadership styles, reflecting the complexity and adaptability required in effective leadership.

Appendix

Resources for Enhancing Your HQ

Books

1. **"Start With Why"** by Simon Sinek: This insightful book delves into the concept of purpose and its role in driving successful organizations and leaders. Sinek argues that the most successful companies and leaders start by asking 'why' - why they exist, why they do what they do - and this 'why' guides all their actions and decisions. This aligns closely with the cognitive dimension of HQ, particularly the aspect of proactive thinking. By starting with 'why', leaders can think more proactively, make strategic decisions that align with their purpose, and inspire others to follow them.

2. **"Emotional Intelligence"** by Daniel Goleman: In this groundbreaking book, Goleman explores the concept of emotional intelligence and its importance in life and leadership. He argues that emotional intelligence - the ability to understand and manage our own emotions and the emotions of others - is a key determinant of success. This aligns with the behavioural dimension of HQ, particularly the aspect of emotional regulation. By developing emotional intelligence, leaders can better manage their own emotions, respond effectively to the emotions of others, and navigate the emotional dynamics of their teams and organizations.

3. **"How to Win Friends and Influence People"** by Dale Carnegie: This classic book provides practical advice on building relationships and influencing others. Carnegie

offers timeless principles for understanding others, building strong relationships, and influencing people in a positive way. This aligns with the interpersonal dimension of HQ. By applying Carnegie's principles, leaders can build strong, positive relationships with a wide range of stakeholders, foster collaboration and teamwork, and influence others towards shared goals.

4. **"7 Habits of Highly Effective People"** by Stephen Covey: Stephen R. Covey's "7 Habits of Highly Effective People" is a pivotal guide for anyone aspiring to be a proactive leader. It emphasizes aligning actions with core values of integrity and fairness, fostering effective leadership across personal and professional spheres. Covey's work advocates for initiative, goal setting, effective prioritization, and the importance of mutual understanding and collaboration. This book is a key resource for developing a leadership approach that is ethical, impactful, and sustainable, equipping leaders to navigate complexities with resilience and foster a culture of growth and respect.

5. **"The Power Within"** by Anurag Rai: The book teaches 21 different ways to meditate and also provides scientific evidence of why you should meditate, and how meditation will help you become a better husband or wife, a better parent, a better friend, and a better leader. Most people fail in meditation because they tried one approach, and it did not work for them. This book introduces 21 different meditation formats put together as a 21-day meditation challenge.

6. **"Mind 2.0 ~ A deeper understanding of human mind and it's true potential"** by Anurag Rai: This book is highly recommended by the author as everything in leadership is about understanding and managing people. People are driven by two faculties emotion and reason. Both are an output of mind. Therefore, to understand people we must understand human mind.

Online Resources

1. <u>Mindfulness Apps</u>: In today's fast-paced world, mindfulness apps like Headspace and Calm provide an accessible way to practice mindfulness and enhance emotional regulation, a key aspect of the behavioural dimension of HQ. These apps offer guided meditations, mindfulness exercises, and educational resources to help you cultivate mindfulness, manage stress, and improve emotional regulation.

2. <u>Online Courses</u>: Websites like Coursera and Udemy offer a wealth of online courses on a wide range of topics relevant to HQ. You can find courses on strategic thinking, emotional intelligence, effective communication, leadership styles, and much more. These courses, often taught by experts in the field, provide valuable knowledge and practical strategies to enhance your HQ. They also offer the flexibility to learn at your own pace, in your own time. If you want a personalised training program to enhance your team's HQ get in touch with us at info@amhwal.com.

3. <u>TED Talks</u>: TED.com is a treasure trove of short, impactful talks on a wide range of topics. You can find talks on everything from the science of emotions to the art of leadership. These talks can provide fresh insights, inspire new ideas, and challenge your thinking, all of which can contribute to enhancing your HQ. Some recommended talks include Simon Sinek's "Start With

Why", Daniel Goleman's talk on emotional intelligence, and Brene Brown's talks on vulnerability and empathy.

Workshops and Seminars

Enhancing an organization's Human Quotient (HQ) involves developing the emotional intelligence, interpersonal skills, and overall well-being of its members. This can lead to improved communication, collaboration, and a more positive workplace culture. Here are several workshops or training sessions that can help in enhancing your organization's HQ:

1. **Emotional Intelligence Training**: Focused on helping participants understand and manage their own emotions, as well as recognize and influence the emotions of others. This training can cover topics such as self-awareness, self-regulation, motivation, empathy, and social skills.

2. **Effective Communication Workshops**: These workshops can teach employees how to communicate clearly and effectively, both verbally and non-verbally. They can include elements of active listening, assertive communication, feedback techniques, and conflict resolution.

3. **Team Building and Collaboration**: Designed to improve teamwork skills, such sessions can include activities that foster trust, mutual respect, and cooperation

among team members. They can also teach how to leverage diverse strengths and perspectives for team success.

4. **Mindfulness and Well-being Programs**: Training in mindfulness can help employees manage stress, improve focus, and enhance overall well-being. These programs might include mindfulness meditation, yoga, or other stress-reduction techniques.

5. **Leadership Development Programs**: Aimed at developing emotional intelligence and people skills among leaders, these programs can cover topics like visionary leadership, coaching skills, influence without authority, and creating psychologically safe environments.

6. **Diversity and Inclusion Training**: Essential for fostering an inclusive workplace where every member feels valued and understood. Topics can include unconscious bias, cultural competence, inclusive leadership, and strategies for building a diverse and inclusive team.

7. **Conflict Resolution and Negotiation**: Teaching employees how to effectively manage and resolve conflicts can lead to a more harmonious workplace. Training can include negotiation skills, understanding different conflict styles, and strategies for finding common ground.

8. **Feedback and Performance Coaching**: Workshops that teach how to give and receive feedback constructively can enhance growth and performance. Coaching skills for managers can also be included, focusing on how to

support employee development through effective feedback and guidance.

When selecting workshops or trainings, consider the specific needs of your organization and its members. Tailoring the content and approach to your organizational context will make these initiatives more impactful. It's also beneficial to integrate these trainings into a broader strategy of organizational development, ensuring that they are not one-off events but part of a continuous effort to enhance your organization's human quotient.

At AMHWAL Academy, we recognize the unique needs of your organization in enhancing its Human Quotient. That's why we offer customized programs combining workshops and trainings tailored to your specific goals. Our team works closely with you to identify your team's strengths and growth areas, designing a bespoke program that not only meets your current needs but also supports your long-term success. From improving emotional intelligence to developing leadership skills, AMHWAL Academy delivers a targeted approach to elevate your team and leadership's capabilities, ensuring lasting organizational growth. Send your enquiry to info@amhwal.com.

Assessment Tools

1. **360-Degree Feedback:** This tool involves collecting feedback from a variety of sources (e.g., superiors, peers, subordinates) to get a comprehensive view of your leadership skills. It can provide valuable insights into your cognitive, behavioural, and interpersonal skills, and highlight areas for improvement. Many organizations offer 360-degree feedback as part of their leadership development programs.

2. **Emotional Intelligence Assessments:** Tools like the Emotional Quotient Inventory (EQ-i) can help you understand and improve your emotional regulation skills. These assessments typically measure various aspects of emotional intelligence, including self-awareness, emotional regulation, empathy, and interpersonal skills. They can provide a detailed profile of your emotional intelligence, highlight strengths and areas for improvement, and provide targeted strategies for enhancing your emotional regulation skills.

3. **Myers-Briggs Type Indicator (MBTI):** While not directly measuring HQ, the MBTI can provide insights into your personality, which can inform your approach to enhancing your HQ. The MBTI measures preferences in how people perceive the world and make decisions, and can provide insights into your natural strengths, potential challenges, and preferred leadership style.

4. **AMHWAL Leadership Style assessment:** AMHWAL Leadership Style Assessment Tool is a streamlined solution designed to identify and understand diverse leadership styles. This intuitive tool evaluates leaders through targeted questions, revealing their predominant leadership approach, be it transformative, transactional, servant, or participative. The assessment offers insightful feedback, enabling leaders to align their style with organizational goals and team needs. It serves as a foundation for targeted development strategies, enhancing leadership effectiveness and fostering a culture of adaptive leadership. With AMHWAL's assessment, leaders can refine their approach for maximum impact and organizational growth. Send your enquiry to info@amhwal.com

5. **AMHWAL Personality Test:** AMHWAL Personality Assessment Tool is a precise instrument designed to uncover the intricate layers of an individual's personality traits and how they influence leadership and workplace dynamics. This tool leverages scientifically validated frameworks to provide a deep dive into personality dimensions, offering personalized insights that empower individuals to leverage their strengths and address potential challenges. The assessment facilitates a deeper understanding of personal and interpersonal work styles, enhancing team collaboration and leadership effectiveness. With AMHWAL's tool, leaders and teams gain the clarity needed to drive personal growth and organizational success. Send your enquiry to info@amhwal.com.

6. **AMHWAL 360 Feedback + Coaching:** AMHWAL Academy offers an Executive Coaching Service combining 360-degree feedback with personalized coaching to enhance leadership skills. This service includes comprehensive feedback collection from a broad stakeholder base, detailed analysis, and tailored executive coaching sessions. Leaders receive a custom development plan based on feedback insights, focusing on strengths and areas for improvement. Our experienced coaches guide leaders through actionable strategies for growth, fostering self-awareness and organizational impact. This condensed approach ensures leaders not only understand their performance from multiple perspectives but also receive the support needed to achieve measurable improvements in leadership effectiveness. Send your enquiry to info@amhwal.com.

Further Guides and Resources for Effective Leadership

Time Management

EAT THAT FROG

This principle suggests starting your day by tackling the most challenging task first. This approach emphasizes productivity by handling difficult tasks when your energy and focus are at their peak

POMODORO

This Technique involves working in focused, 25-minute intervals (called Pomodoros) followed by a 5-minute break. After four Pomodoros, take a longer break. This method boosts productivity and prevents burnout by balancing work and rest.

TIME BLOCKING

Time blocking is a time management method where you divide your day into blocks of time. Each block is dedicated to accomplishing a specific task or group of tasks. This approach helps in organizing your schedule efficiently and focusing better on tasks.

Tuesday
Task group 1
9 - 11
Task group 2
12 - 14
Task group 3
15 - 17

GETTING THINGS DONE

GTD is a method where tasks are recorded externally and broken down into actionable work items. It involves organizing items in a systematic way to focus on the right task at the right time, enhancing efficiency and reducing mental load.

PICKLE JAR THEORY

It likens your day to a jar, filled first with big 'rocks' (important tasks), then pebbles (smaller tasks), and finally sand (trivial activities). This illustrates prioritizing significant tasks to ensure productivity and effective time use.

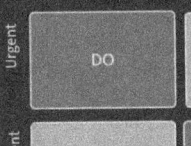

EISENHOWER MATRIX

A tool for prioritizing tasks by urgency and importance. It divides tasks into four quadrants: urgent and important, important but not urgent, urgent but not important, and neither urgent nor important. This helps in deciding which tasks to focus on, schedule, delegate, or eliminate.

 superhumaninyou.com   amhwal.com

Psychological Safety
The Ultimate Cheat Sheet

Amy Edmondson's Psychological safety model

↑ HIGH — PSYCHOLOGICAL SAFETY — LOW ↓

COMFORT ZONE
People feel safe and comfortable, but there's little incentive to achieve results, leading to a pleasant yet unproductive environment.

LEARNING ZONE
The ideal balance where team members feel safe to take risks and express ideas, while also being responsible for their performance, fostering a dynamic and productive environment.

APATHY ZONE
Team members are disengaged and unmotivated, doing the bare minimum without a sense of responsibility or freedom to express ideas.

ANXIETY ZONE
High pressure and stress prevail as team members are held accountable but fear speaking up or making mistakes, stifling innovation.

← LOW — PERFORMANCE STANDARDS — HIGH →

6 ways Leaders can create Psychological Safety in their Teams

1. **Encourage Open Communication**
   Leaders should create a culture where team members feel comfortable voicing their thoughts, questions, and concerns without fear of ridicule or reprisal.

2. **Show Empathy and Understanding**
   Leaders must show that they understand and care about the concerns and well-being of their team members.

3. **Promote a Learning Mindset**
   Leaders should emphasize the importance of learning from mistakes rather than penalizing them.

4. **Give Constructive Feedback**
   Feedback should be aimed at helping team members grow and improve. A leader might regularly schedule one-on-one meetings with team members to discuss their progress

5. **Lead by Example**
   If a leader wants their team to be open and honest, they must also be transparent about their own challenges and learning experiences.

6. **Foster Inclusivity and Diversity**
   Leaders must ensure that all team members, regardless of their background or job role, feel included and valued.

amhwal.com   Anurag Rai

4 CORE SELF-EVALUATIONS

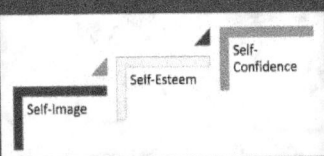

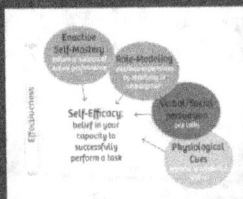

Self-Esteem: This reflects how much you value and respect yourself. High self-esteem equips you with confidence to face challenges and believe in your abilities to succeed.

Self-Efficacy: This is about your belief in your ability to perform tasks successfully. It's a powerful predictor of goal setting, motivation, and performance in the workplace.

@Anurag Rai

@Anurag Rai

SELF ESTEEM | **SELF EFFICACY**

EMOTIONAL STABILITY | **LOCUS OF CONTROL**

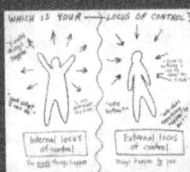

Emotional Stability: This involves maintaining a calm and composed demeanor, even in stressful situations. It enables you to make rational decisions and keep your emotions in check.

Locus of Control: Do you believe that you control your destiny, or is it controlled by external factors? A strong internal locus of control empowers you to take charge of your actions and their outcomes.

Download a high-res pdf colour copy of this doc at AMHWAL.COM/RESOURCES

5 PSYCHOLOGY CONCEPTS TO HELP YOU BECOME A BETTER LEADER AND MANAGER

1. Maslow's Hierarchy of Needs: Understanding that people have different levels of needs, from basic (like food and shelter) to higher-level (like esteem and self-actualization), can help in motivating and engaging team members.

2. The Pygmalion Effect: Higher expectations (seeing higher potential) from your team members lead to an increase in their performance. People internalize others' expectations, influencing their behaviour.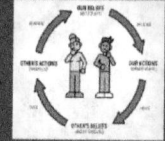

3. Locus of Control: Some people believe they have control over events (internal locus of control), while others feel external forces dictate outcomes (external locus of control). Recognizing these orientations can help leaders tailor their approach.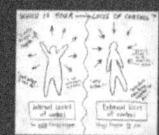

4. Self-efficacy: The belief in one's ability to achieve specific outcomes largely dictates one's performance and so the outcome. Enhancing the self-efficacy of your team can boost performance and motivation.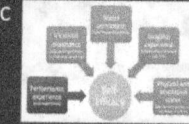

5. Groupthink: In decision-making, leaders should be cautious about this phenomenon where the desire for harmony and conformity results in poor decisions, suppressing dissent and alternative viewpoints.

© Anurag Rai

By understanding and leveraging these psychological concepts, leaders can better manage, motivate, and inspire their teams, ultimately leading to more effective and harmonious workplaces.

Download high res pdf colour copy of this doc at AMHWAL.COM/RESOURCES

EMOTIONAL INTELLIGENCE (EQ)
The Ultimate one page guide for busy leaders

DEFINITION

Emotional Intelligence (EI) refers to the ability of a leader to recognize, understand, and manage their own emotions as well as those of others.

THE FOUR ELEMENTS OF EQ

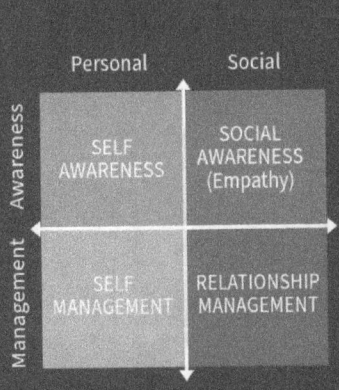

1. **Self-Awareness:** This is the ability to recognize and understand one's own emotions, strengths, weaknesses, values, and drivers, and how they affect others.

2. **Self-Management:** This involves controlling or redirecting one's disruptive emotions and adapting to changing circumstances.

3. **Social Awareness (Empathy):** This is the ability to understand the emotions, needs, and concerns of other people, pick up on emotional cues, feel comfortable socially, and recognize the power dynamics in a group or organization.

4. **Relationship Management:** This refers to the ability to manage interactions with others, inspiring and influencing them. It includes developing and maintaining good relationships, communicating clearly, inspiring and influencing others, working well in a team, and managing conflict.

FOUR WAYS TO IMPROVE YOUR EQ

 Enhance self-awareness by reflecting on emotions and seeking feedback.

 Boost social awareness with active listening and empathy.

 Develop self-regulation through mindfulness and pausing before reacting.

Improve relationship management via effective communication and positive conflict resolution.

Having a high EQ is not about being nice all the time,. It is also not about controling, or manipulating emotions. Instead it is about understanding and managing emotions with kindness and in a way that leads to positive outcome for both people and the business

 superhumaninyou.com   amhwal.com

9 MOST POPULAR TED TALKS ON LEADERSHIP

TOPIC	SPEAKER	# of VIEWS
How great leaders inspire action	Simon Sinek	63.8M
The surprising habits of original thinkers	Adam Grant	21.5M
Why good leaders make you feel safe	Simon Sinek	19.5M
Why we have too few women leaders	Sheryl Sandberg	11.9M
How to start a movement	Derek Sivers	10.5M
Are you a giver or a taker	Adam Grant	10.2M
Why I'm done trying to be "man enough"	Justin Baldoni	8.5M
Why the secret to success is setting the right goals	John Doerr	8.4M
Why you think you're right -- even if you're wrong	Julia Galef	7.9M

Download a high-res pdf of this doc and more resources like this at AMHWAL.COM/RESOURCES

△ AMHWAL Academy

Download a high-res pdf colour copy of this doc at AMHWAL.COM/RESOURCES

FRAMEWORKS TO GIVE CONSTRUCTIVE FEEDBACK

THE 3 P'S MODEL

PRAISE — Highlight something positive
Example: "Great job on finishing the project ahead of schedule; your efficiency is impressive!"

PROBLEM — Identify & Explain the issue without blaming
Example: "However, there were some errors in the data analysis that need attention."

PLAN — Suggest solutions to overcome the problem.
Example: "Let's review the analysis together, and I'll show you how to avoid such mistakes in the future."

HARVARD'S HEAR FRAMEWORK

HEAR — Actively listen to the concerns raised by the other person without interruption.
Example: A team member explains they're struggling with their workload.

EMPATHIZE — Show understanding and validate the other person's feelings and experiences.
Example: "I can understand how the workload might be overwhelming for you."

ACKNOWLEDGE — Recognize the issue and its impact without necessarily agreeing or disagreeing.
"I acknowledge that the current project has put extra pressure on you."

RESPOND — Provide feedback, potential solutions, or a plan to address the concerns raised.
Example: "Let's explore how we might redistribute some tasks to manage the workload better."

THE SBI MODEL

SITUATION — Describe the occasion when the behaviour occurred
Example: "During yesterday's team meeting."

BEHAVIOUR — Explain the actual action or behaviour of the individual.
Example: "You interrupted colleagues while they were speaking."

IMPACT — Share the effect that the behaviour had on you or others.
Example: "which made some team members feel unheard and frustrated."

BONUS TIP

Make more deposits
Than withdrawals

Every praise is like a deposit, and every constructive feedback is like a withdrawal for an individual's emotional bank account.

ADHERE TO A 5:1 RATIO

A good practice to always have a nice rapport with your team is to make a habit of giving 5 praises every day to every person who works directly with you.

Download a high-res pdf colour copy of this doc at AMHWAL.COM/RESOURCES

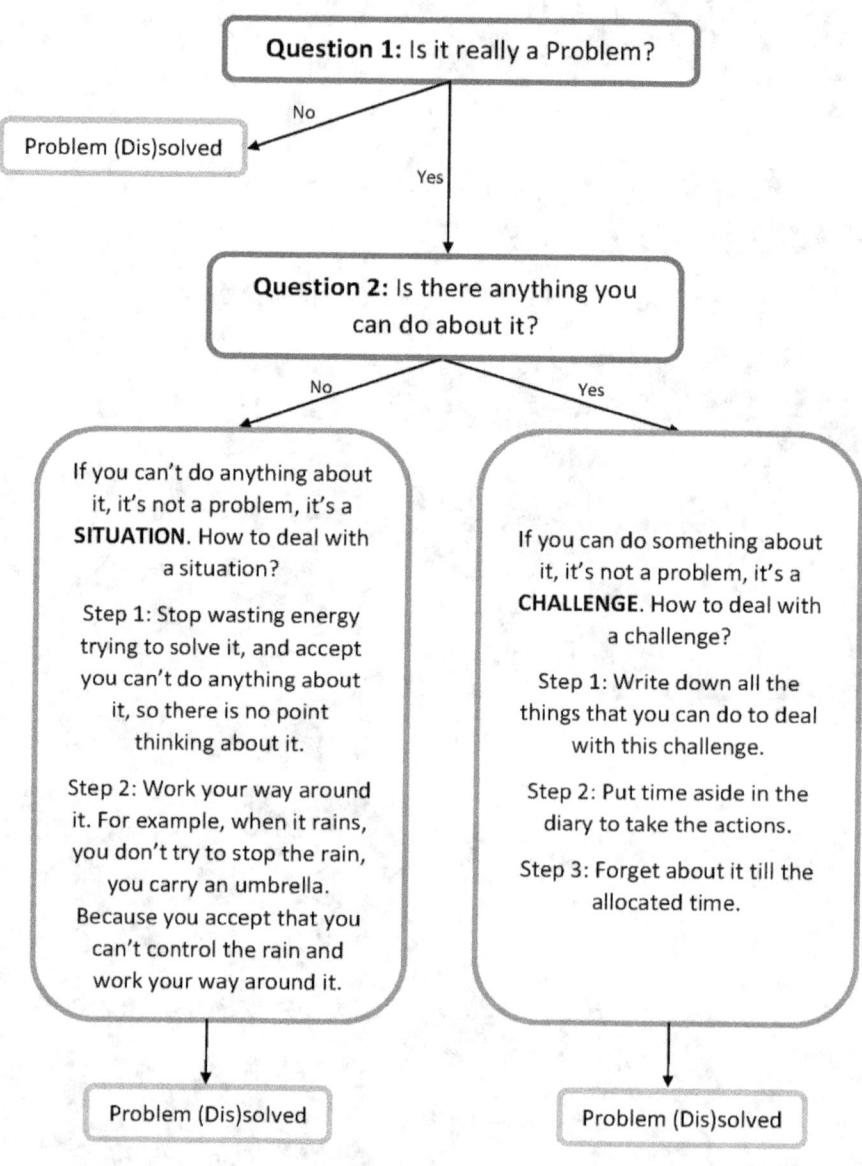

www.ingramcontent.com/pod-product-compliance
Lightning Source LLC
Chambersburg PA
CBHW052159220526
45471CB00004B/1738